AMERICAN INDIANS:

A STUDY GUIDE AND SOURCEBOOK

by

Lynn P. Dunn

San Francisco
1975

Printed in 1975

by

R and E Research Associates
4843 Mission St., San Francisco 94112
18581 McFarland Ave., Saratoga, CA 95070

Publishers and Distributors of Ethnic Studies
Editor: Adam S. Eterovich
Publisher: Robert D. Reed

Library of Congress Card Catalog Number

74-31618

ISBN

0-88247-305-0

Dedication

To Rupert Weeks, Ross Morres and Tom Shakespeare,
whose generosity, insight and warmth as teachers and as
friends are appreciated.

Acknowledgments

I am grateful to Glenn Alleman and Michael Juarez, teachers who worked with me, in good faith though much too hastily, in late fall and early winter of 1970-1971, to construct the Native American portion of an interim ethnic studies guide for teachers in Clark County, Nevada, and to Bill Moore and Robert Dunsheath for the support they gave that project. From the resulting document, printed in looseleaf form in January of 1971, I have borrowed some ideas for this volume.

I am indebted also to John Cebular, who worked with me during the spring of 1971 to improve that insubstantial guide, and to Ross Morres of Nevada's Indian Affairs Commission and to Carolyn Wright of the newspaper Native Nevadan, who generously gave of their time and their knowledge to help us that spring.

University of Illinois Professors J. N. Hook, Alan Purves and Keneth Kinnamon read early versions of this volume and made suggestions which, so far as I have been successful in following them, have improved the proportion and content of this book. Their encouragement and help have been invaluable.

Thanks also to my Native American students at University of Wyoming--such as Eugene Goggles and Ernie Whiteman, whose leadership of Keepers of the Fire I have admired, and the Wind River Teacher Corps Interns--for sharing experiences and insights with me.

L. D.

Table of Contents

Introduction

This book is one of a four volume series on American minorities (one volume each on Blacks, Chicanos, Native Americans, and Asian Americans). In each volume three themes are treated: Identity, Conflict, and Integration/ Nationalism. Each volume may serve in itself as a text or guide for the student or teacher in the study of a particular minority. The organization of each volume in the same thematic way may lead the reader to important points of comparison or contrast among the four minorities treated in the series.

Though any study of ethnicity in America will probably deal with white racism, it is not the intention here to suggest that Whites have monopoly on racism or injustice. One may look elsewhere for examples: to the long history of the Jews in many lands and among many peoples; to the persecutions involved in various religious movements; to the Tlaxcaltecas and other Indian tribes who had been subjugated by the Aztecs, and who in turn aided the Spanish invaders in the destruction of their masters; and, more recently, to events in Nigeria, Bangladesh, or in some countries in South America where there have been gross examples of nationalistic chauvinism at the expense of indigenous peoples. No group or society (or even so-called "classless society") seems immune; all humans are potentially victims and persecutors.

These volumes document white racism and some of the problems and struggles minorities have faced (and continue to experience) in the United States. There are other elements of importance which are treated as well: the personal contributions of individuals, and the richness and texture added to American culture by minority groups.

To maintain a sense of objectivity (not that total objectivity is claimed), the practice in writing these volumes has generally been to let events speak for themselves without editorializing. For the sake of objectivity, and to aid the reader in his own search for understanding, sources included for further study quite often represent several viewpoints (some of them bigoted or extremist, on one or more sides of an issue).

Within a given thematic section of each volume, the study outline is basically historical and chronological in development. The aim in each text, though, is to provide the reader a many-dimensioned, cross-disciplinary study experience, with a heavy stress upon humanistic concerns. For example, there is probably more emphasis upon literary sources than upon historical incident or fact in the "Notes and Sources" column of a given volume.

The "Notes and Sources" column provides references to sources which bear upon, and notes which deal with sidelights to--or which expand upon-- the parallel "Study Outline." Though most of the sources cited for further study bear directly and importantly upon the study outline, at times a source is given which is merely allusive.

This brief volume is not an exhaustive study, nor does its bibliography contain a complete list of the many publications relevant to American Indian Studies. Rather, this book is intended to serve as a beginning reference text for students and teachers. It should provide a sufficiently broad scope and adequate references for a solid foundation upon which to build. The teacher or student who finds this volume to be a useful tool or text, will, through further study (to which this text may point the way or help the reader find his own direction), discover aspects of Native American Studies which are not treated here and will find additional important sources for study.

PART ONE: AMERICAN INDIAN IDENTITY

I   Introduction

Indian America has produced great statesmen and orators, profound thinkers, artists and poets, superb athletes, and unsurpassed military tacticians and warriors. Though most American are familiar with a few Indian names from history, such as Squanto and Pocahontas, most are unfamiliar with the consistently high quality of Indian military leaders or with the qualities of Indian culture.

Many Whites know Indians from the movies or television, where the Indian rides rapidly off camera when the cavalry bugle is heard from the far horizon. To many Whites the Indian is known only in some combination of stereotypes.

The stereotypes range to impossible extremes. On the one hand is the noble savage, proudly silent, perfectly honorable, in tune with nature, incredibly keen of hearing and eyesight, and able to run all day without tiring, or to ride the wildest horse. His feminine counterpart is always slender and beautiful, perfectly chaste and of royal blood--a "princess" (in a society with no kings!)

The other extreme holds that the Indian is dirty, bloodthirsty, stupid, malicious, lazy, and drunken, and that the Indian survives only by courtesy of generous Whites. At this extreme the Indian woman becomes a "squaw" of dubious morals and of untidy personal habits, who does all the work while her "buck" loafs.

In fact, Indians are human beings, and like all men cannot be neatly captured in stereotyped descriptions, although individual Indians (or Whites) could be found who have characteristics which fit some of the stereotypes.

II   Guide and Sourcebook

Study Outline	*Notes and Sources*
A. Indians in what is now the United States developed rich and interesting cultures of their own.	
1. In the New England area, the Iroquois confederation of the five tribes had	(The five tribes: Cayugas, Mohawks, Oneidas, Onondagas and Senecas)

Study Outline	*Notes and Sources*

a remarkable culture.

a. The early leader Hiawatha, whom the Iroquois revered, had preached to his people of universal peace, of the equality and brotherhood of all mankind.

Josephy, "The Real Hiawatha," The Patriot Chiefs

Sanders and Peek, Literature of the American Indian (Chapter 4)

b. Many of the Iroquois standards of moral conduct were based on the teachings of Hiawatha.

c. Iroquois leaders were noted for their imaginative thinking, their logic and intelligence, and their persuasive oratory.

Murphy, "Silence, the Word, and Indian Rhetoric," College Composition and Communication, XXI (December 1960) (This article has several brief examples of notable Indian orations.)

d. Iroquois "wampum" had a much greater significance than is usually attached to the term. Wampum strands or belts served as a substitute for written language. The colored beads which were fashioned from shells were fashioned in various designs and symbols which had specific meanings.

(The Keeper of the Wampum was able to "read" from the strings and belts of past occurrences of importance and binding treaties or alliances, which different shell patterns recorded.)

e. Cadwallader Colden, who wrote a history of the Iroquois in 1727, remarked of the Iroquois governmental system:

(See also "The Law of the Great Peace of the People of the Longhouse" in Sanders and Peek's Literature of the American Indian)

Each Nation is an absolute Re-
publick by its self, govern'd in
all Publick Affairs of War and
Peace by the Sachems or Old Men,
whose Authority and Power is gain'd
by and consists wholly in the
Opinion the rest of the Nation have
of their Wisdom and Integrity.
They never execute their Resolu-
tions by Compulsion or Force upon
any of their people. Honor and
Esteem are their Principal Rewards,
as Shame & being Despised are their
Punishments.

f. In 1754 Benjamin Franklin's proposed Albany Plan of Union for the
colonies drew direct inspiration
from Hiawatha's League. In part
the political institutions of the
League lived on in new governments
white men were establishing for
themselves, though the Iroquois
lost most of their strength in the
military defeat they suffered in
the Revolutionary War.

Porter, The Battle of the 1,000
Slain (Chapter 1)
(Throughout the Eighteenth Century
the republican and democratic prin-
ciples of the Five Nations' system
of government were studied by men
of learning.)

2. The Plains Indians culture underwent
a remarkable change with acquisition
of the horse. Young men learned to
ride and became expert horsemen
(their elders were more conservative). In one generation the Plains
Indians became more mobile and more
competent in obtaining buffalo.

Grinnell, The Fighting Cheyennes
Grinnell, Pawnee Hero Stories
and Folk Tales
Neihardt, Black Elk Speaks
Parsons, American Indian Life
Momaday, The Way to Rainy Mountain
(sensitively written book on Kiowa
legends, myths and history)

a. Their method of hunting went from the cautious stalk to the rapid chase.

b. The horse also became a prize for raiding parties, as young men practiced the art of surprise attack and quick withdrawal.

Roe, The Indian and the Horse

c. Plains Indian life was permeated by a religious sense of unity with the world of the tribe and earth, plants and animals.

Hamilton, Cry of the Thunderbird (Writings of Indians on aspects of culture, customs, adventure)

3. The Pueblo and Hopi tribes of the Southwest developed citadels on tops of mesas for protection from raiding Apaches and Navajos.

a. The rich cultures of these people included elaborate myths and re-ligious ceremonies.

Waters, Book of the Hopi
Waters, Pumpkin Seed Point
(Waters stresses the importance of myth and symbolism.)

b. Unlike some other Indian tribes, the Hopi and Pueblo groups prac-ticed an elaborate food storage program in order to exist through cycles of drought in their arid lands.

O'Kane, Sun in the Sky (Hopis and Pueblos, expert farmers in their desert lands, developed remarkably productive strains of corn and other vegetables and fruits.)

Study Outline	_Notes and Sources_

c. Zunis and other Pueblos and the Hopis developed distinctive craftsmanship in pottery, weaving, and jewelry making.

Vogt and Albert, <u>People of Rimrock</u>

4. The Paiutes of Nevada developed a cultural system adapted to the demands of their homeland.

Hopkins, <u>Life Among the Piutes</u>

a. The economy was based on a combination of hunting, planting, and gathering.

Forbes, <u>Nevada Indians Speak</u>
Scott, <u>Karnee</u> (Annie Lowry's story--
The commentary by Charles R.

b. Like other tribes, the Paiutes had a rich heritage of myths and legends, passed from generation to generation through memory, which related to religious beliefs and practices.

Craig and the introduction by Robert P. Heizer are useful notes on history and culture of Nevada Indians.)
Wheat, <u>Survival Arts of the Primitive Paiutes</u> (Mrs. Topsy

c. Moving with the seasons, to hunting or gathering grounds (for pine nuts or other seeds) and then back to watered oases, the Paiutes lived an interesting though sometimes hard life in the Great Basin.

Swain, a Southern Nevada Paiute, is one of the few living who are skilled in traditional crafts of the Paiute culture.)

B. Literature, the arts, and religion were integral parts of Indian life.

Study Outline	*Notes and Sources*
1. American Indians had distinct literary traditions. Often poetry and myths were associated with religion.	Sanders and Peek, Literature of the American Indian
a. Indians living in what is now Mexico consciously developed poetry traditions, which were different from but not inferior to European poetic traditions. Extant Nahua poems show an imaginative use of image and metaphor. Aztec poems have sophisticated poetic themes; a number of them are prophetic in nature.	Day, "Mayas and Aztecs of Ancient Mexico," The Sky Clears (an especially good section) Leon-Portilla, Pre-Columbian Literatures of Mexico
b. Religious expression and ceremony of nearly all American Indians had a symbolic and literary quality.	Neihardt, Black Elk Speaks (This book can provide a moving personal experience for the advanced student who can approach it with respect for the Sioux medicine man and prophet, Black Elk.)
d. The ghost dance religious movement, which began in Nevada, inspired a number of Indian poets.	Day, "Songs of the Ghost Dance Religion," The Sky Clears ("The Whirlwind," a Paiute poem or song, envisions the new earth.)
e. Many of the traditional myths which passed on in an oral tradition from generation to generation had religious significance. A number of them were very similar to some of the classic Greek myths.	Clark, Indian Legends from the Northern Rockies

Study Outline	*Notes and Sources*
f. Several observers noted that the storytellers among the Indians had developed oral traditions quite similar to the oral storytelling traditions of medieval Europe or of Greece.	Sanders and Peek, Literature of the American Indian Irving, Astoria (Washington Irving noted the improvisational style of Indian storytellers as they chanted of hunting and of war, occasionally indulging in comic humor or dry satire.)
2. Indian art developed to reflect tradition and the artist's own imaginative grasp of his universe.	
a. Traditional Indian art reflected the religious beliefs and the way of life of the tribe; the unity of tribal culture was reflected in art as well as literature.	Neihardt, Black Elk Speaks (Note the relationship between paintings and religious experience.) Waters, Book of the Hopi (Waters treats the Jungian significance of Hopi art and the relationship of art to religion.)
b. Indian art is often symbolic or impressionistic rather than simply objective.	Momaday, The Way to Rainy Mountain (Al Momaday's illustrations are good examples.)
c. Practical objects of Indian life are often characterized by design and craftsmanship which give them value as art objects. Some examples are Iroquois wampum belts, masks and dress; baskets and pottery of many tribes; jewelry of the Pueblos, Hopis, Navajos, and others; saddles and bridles; bead	(Dorothy Dunn and others have written extensively on Indian artists and art and on traditional and modern tribal crafts.)

Study Outline	*Notes and Sources*
and quill work in costumes; rugs and other woven objects.	
d. The Institute of American Indian Arts, under the direction of Lloyd New, is currently engaged in training young Indians in the arts.	Brody, Indian Painters and White Patrons
3. Religion was (and still is in many cases) a central unifying force in tribal life. Though many tribes had religions which were very similar, there was also as much or perhaps more variety in Indian religions as in Christian religions, for example.	Neihardt, Black Elk Speaks (Sioux holy man's personal account of his revelations, his successes, failures.) Waters, Book of the Hopi and Pumpkin Seed Point (Waters reveals details of Hopi religious beliefs and practices and comments on the validity of Hopi religion.)
a. It is important to remember that the Indian holds his religion to be sacred; he does not wish what he regards as holy to be paraded out for public inspection and made light of.	Wilson, Apologies to the Iroquois Udall, Me and Mine (Helen Sekaquaptewa talks about similarities between Hopi and Mormon beliefs.)
b. Indians believed in observing the Counsel of living prophets. Holy men were consulted on many crucial points: sickness, warfare, and other serious personal or tribal matters.	Grinnell, "A Story of Faith," Pawnee Hero Stories and Folk Tales LaFarge, The Enemy Gods (The novel's main character is caught between his Navajo beliefs and

Study Outline	Notes and Sources
c. Much of Plains Indian religion centered around several lodges (such as the offerings lodge or sun dance lodge), each of which had particular responsibilities within the tribal religion, including the transmission of tribal culture.	the Christian teachings of boarding school.) Mendoza, "Summer Water and Shirley," in Momaday's American Indian Authors (This story illustrates the strength of belief.) Parsons, American Indian Life Mooney, The Ghost Dance Religion Benjamin Franklin, excerpt from
d. Generally, Indians had a deep reverence for all life, holding that all living things were intelligent. (Such a belief caused them to give a respect to animals which Whites did not understand; it also caused them to expect more from their animals than Whites did. And it seemed that the animals responded; witness the rides Joseph's Nez Percés and Dull Knife's Cheyennes made on ponies eating only grass while their pursuers continually threw new men on "superior," fresh, corn-fed horses against them.)	Concerning the Savages of North America, in Anderson and Wright's The Dark and Tangled Path Littlebird, "Death in the Woods," in Momaday's American Indian Authors Momaday, "The Bear and the Colt," in Momaday's American Indian Authors Waters, Man Who Killed the Deer (In Momaday and Waters, hunters show reverence for the animals they kill.)
e. Some Indian religions preached a fleshly immortality for men and	Cohoe, "The Promised Visit," in Momaday's American Indian Authors

Study Outline	Notes and Sources

animals. (White Christians, who
seemed to be ashamed of their
bodies, regarded such a doctrine
as pagan and heretical and "inferior.") The Ghost Dancers ex-
pected their ancestors and the
herds of dead buffalo to return.

f. Indian religions made demands upon
adherents. Young men went on
lonely retreats, fasting and
praying for personal revelation.
Warriors of the Plains Indians
sometimes swung at the pole in the
sundance ritual to gain honor and
inspiration through suffering.

g. To many Indians the manner of death
was very important. To die in
battle was honorable. To die
"well" was terribly important.

h. To the Indian his religion was a
very serious thing, to be prac-
ticed and observed at all times as
an integral part of his whole existence. His personal medicine
must be observed as well as taboos
and practices which religion

(An interesting ghost-love
story involving a young man's
acceptance of traditional
Navajo beliefs about the dead.)
(See also the Arapaho "Over the
Hill" account in Marriott and
Rachlin's American Indian
Mythology.)
Seattle, "Dead, Did I Say? There
Is No Death," in Witt and
Steiner's The Way
Johnson, A Man Called Horse
(There are several relevant
stories in the collection.)

(Torture of captives was regarded
as a means of giving the victim
a chance to die without complaint
despite his pain.)
Blatchford, "Religion of the
People," in Witt and Steiner's
The Way

dictated to the tribe as a group.

C. There are many identity stereotypes which are associated with America's Indians.

Sando, "White Created Myths About the Native American," Indian Historian, IV (Winter 1971)

1. Indians were described as blood-thirsty savages in warfare.

a. When they mutilated bodies in ways which were strange or new to the Whites, they were characterized as barbarians. Following their own customs (which varied from tribe to tribe) some Indians did perform acts of brutality. But wars tend to generate brutality, and Whites are really no less prone to commit obscene acts of violence than anyone else (witness My Lai or Sand Creek).

McGaa, "A Bigoted Textbook," Indian Historian, IV (Fall 1971)
Henry, Textbooks and the American Indian (Stereotypes are noted by Indian scholars.)
"My Teacher Is a Lizard: Education and Culture," in Witt and Steiner's The Way (Contains several selections related to stereotypes.)

b. At the time the Puritans were complaining of Indian atrocities, they were busily engaged in the English custom of quartering some of their own enemies. (King Philip's head was on display for 25 years after his body was decapitated and quartered.)

Colden, The History of the Five Indian Nations (Colden records the torture a young Iroquois prisoner received at the hands of his French captors:

"They first broiled his Feet between two red hot Stones; then they put his Fingers into red hot Pipes,...they cut his Joints, and taking hold of the Sinews, twisted

11

c. It was the Colonies themselves which encouraged the practice of scalping, with Massachusetts offering a hefty bounty of 100 pounds sterling for an Indian scalp in 1724. In 1755 the rates were 40 pounds sterling for the scalp of a male Indian over 12 years of age, and half that amount for the scalp of either a female Indian or a male under 12.

them round small Bars of Iron. All this while he kept singing and recounting his own brave actions against the French. At last they flead his scalp from his Skull, and poured scalding hot Sand upon it; at which Time the Intendant's Lady obtained leave of the Governor to have the Coup-de-grace given...."

d. Indians <u>were</u> often savage in warfare. But there were times when they put their white counterparts to shame. Tecumseh told the English commander, Procter, that he was unfit to command when he permitted the massacre of American prisoners in the War of 1812. Tecumseh personally interceded to save the lives of a number of Americans when Procter was again permitting their slaughter.

Josephy, "Tecumseh, the Greatest Indian," The Patriot Chiefs "The Ritual of Death: War and Peace," in Witt and Steiner's The Way (Several selections reflect modern Indian soldiers' concern with the morality of the war in Vietnam.)

e. Indians <u>were</u> often more efficient warriors than the American troops sent out after them. According to

(Officers who thought lightly of Indian fighting abilities were inclined to lead their men into

12

Stanley Vestal, the Plains Indians were extraordinary warriors:	disaster, Fetterman, Grattan and Custer, for example.)
"...figures show that the Sioux killed about five times as many soldiers as he lost Indians killed .... The Indian, Sioux or Cheyenne, was approximately four or five times as effective as the white soldier."	Collier, The Indians of the Americas

2. Like the stereotypes applied to other groups, those which are often attached to Indians are misleading. Indians are described as drunken, dirty, lazy, shiftless, improvident, irresponsible, uncivilized, savage (with two varieties: 'noble' and 'bloodthirsty'), and pagan or heathen. In one sense or another most of these adjectives are true. But they are true of individuals rather than of Indians (they are also true of individual Whites as well).

Standing Bear, "What the Indian Means to America," in Anderson and Wright's The Dark and Tangled Path

Cushman, Stay Away, Joe (Joe in the novel is something of a rascal, likeable perhaps, but not admirable; the others of the family have human frailties, but defy the stereotypes, each in his own way.)

3. Many employers have found Indians to be efficient, hard workers. Indians are as energetic as Whites, though some find it hard to adjust to white American timetables.

Boudinot, "An Address to the Whites," in Anderson and Wright's The Dark and Tangled Path (On stereotypes and Cherokee progress in 1826)

Udall, Me and Mine (Helen Sekaquaptewa's story is not that of a lazy person.)

4. A number of Indians have succumbed to drink. (Whites who become alcoholic

(Some have said that Whites and

Study Outline	*Notes and Sources*

are often less obvious; you may have to look for them to see them.) But many Indians took a path of moderation or total abstinence from liquor.

5. The Indian was regarded by some as a savage beast (the Black had been regarded as a beast of burden). General Francis C. Walker summed up rather well the considerations which shaped some of America's dealings with Indians, in this statement:

> When dealing with savage men, as with savage beasts, no question of national honor can arise. Whether to fight, to run away, or to employ a ruse, is solely a question of expediency.

6. A common criticism for many years was that the Indian was not civilizable because he had no desire to accumulate material possessions. (Almost all Whites wanted more.) American materialism is not so much in vogue at the moment as it was even ten years ago, so there is not the need to defend or apologize for the Indian value system which tended to value a man for the things which he had given

---

Indians made an even trade in their cultural exchange of tobacco and alcohol. It should be pointed out, though, that the Indian's traditional use of tobacco was restricted to ceremonials.)

(For the "noble Savage" treatment, some of Cooper's novels are pertinent.)

Hoffman, excerpt from Greyslaer, in Anderson and Wright's The Dark and Tangled Path (A nineteenth century romantic "noble savage" is portrayed in Hoffman's novel.)

(Some of the social Darwinists were ready to use the Indian's lack of acquisitiveness as another justification for exterminating him.)

(A stingy Navajo may be suspected of Witchcraft.)

Whitecloud, "Blue Winds Dancing," in Momaday's American Indian Authors

away rather than for the possessions

he had amassed.

7. Nineteenth century social Darwinists believed that there were superior or "fitter" groups (specifically White Anglo-Saxons) who should survive at the expense of weaker or inferior peoples (such as the Indians). Extermination of Indians was accepted by them as a logical evolutionary process. Whites were held to be justified in exterminating "weaker" or "inferior" races.

Benton, "The Superiority of the White Race," in Anderson and Wright's The Dark and Tangled Path

Sumner, Social Darwinism

Hofstader, Social Darwinism in American Thought 1860-1915

8. Indians were held to be vagabonds who did not cultivate the soil (hence disobedient to the command in Genesis to "subdue" the earth). It was probably true that few Indians farmed in the manner in which capitalist Americans did in the nineteenth century or do now; yet Indians did plant sufficiently for their needs. They had actually developed many crops which are still basic to American agriculture. Corn, tomatoes, and potatoes originated in the

(The Pilgrims would very likely have lost their lives had not Squanto and others taught them Indian farming methods and supplied them seed.)

O'Kane, Sun in the Sky

Henry, Textbooks and the American Indian (Indians probably contributed more to agriculture as we know it today than did the Europeans.)

Porter, "Prologue: Gifts of the Indian," Battle of the 1,000 Slain

Americas. In addition to these crops
they developed strains of beans,
squashes, melons, cotton and other
crops.

9. Indian medicine men were regarded as
either witches or quacks (or worse)
by Whites. The witchcraft charge
aside, Indians had developed some
successful medical practices. In
fact, prior to the rather remarkable
technological developments and practices of the past hundred years or
so, Indian medical practice was not
inferior to (though it differed from)
that of Europe. A patient probably
stood as good a chance of successful
treatment at the hands of an Indian
medicine man as he did at the hands
of a white American or European doc-
tor prior to mid-nineteenth century.

Hutchens, Indian Herbology of
North America (Some tribes had
sunburn preventatives, insect
repellants, even oral contra-
ceptives.)

Gibbons, Stalking the Wild
Asparagus (Gibbons says,

"Of course, Indian medicine
wasn't entirely free from super-
stition and magic, but, compared
to European medicine of that
day, it looks almost like a
pure empirical science.")

"A Navajo Medicine Man Cures His
Son," in Witt and Steiner's The
Way

10. Indians resent the terms such as
"buck," "brave," "chief," "squaw,"
"papoose," "squawman," "Injun," which
are used to set them apart as
"others." Such terms are often associated with negative stereotypes.

Sanders and Peek, Literature of
the American Indian (Page 184 contains a discussion of the possible
etymology of the word "squaw,"
and the significance of its con-
notations.)

11. Some writers have described Indian languages and Indian speakers as "primitive." Modern linguists have exposed the fallaciousness of such thinking. Sequoyah invented a writing system which was so well constructed that within a very short time the Cherokees had a higher literacy rate than their contemporary 19th century white Americans.

Porter, Battle of the 1,000 Slain (Porter describes Sequoyah as "the only person in the entire history of the world to invent, completely by himself, a simple and practicable alphabet or syllabary.")

Van Every, Disinherited

12. Whites tended to equate Indian systems of government with their own. For instance the colonists, who were used to European institutions, treated the first chiefs they met as if Indians were European monarchs. Governor John Carver kissed Massasoit's hand when they met and immediately negotiated a treaty between the Wampanoags and King James I. Philip, Massasoit's son, became "King Philip" to the colonists, even though the Indian governmental system was actually a democracy.

(During the Indian wars, Whites persistently acted on the assumption that chiefs should be able to control the actions of all their young men, but under Indian forms of government, the young had much greater freedom than Whites gave to their children. Young Indians were advised and occasionally compelled to some action, but generally they were free to go against counsel if they chose.)

13. Some Whites have claimed that Indians are ungrateful for what the

Deloria, Custer Died for Your Sins

government and white people have done for them. "Look at all the land we gave you in your reservations," they may say. The Indian has a greater awareness of what the government and white people have done than those who have such impressions.	Gessner, Massacre (This volume effectively dispels the idea that Indians had become wealthy from government handouts or from their own oil in Oklahoma. Most of the Indians' money never reached Indian hands.)
14. Whites usually associate the Indian with the reservations in the West. The Indian is not associated with city life. Yet Deloria points out that three fourths of America's Indian population lives in cities and in the Eastern United States. Los Angeles has an Indian population of 60,000 or so.	Wilson, Apologies to the Iroquois Deloria, "A Redefinition of Indian Affairs," Custer Died for Your Sins Smith, "The Vanished American," Ensign (July 1971)
15. Indians are often pictured as un-willing or unable to help themselves educationally, yet the historical cultural traditions of Indian educa-tion worked well; and there are fine Indian education programs and in-stitutions and outstanding Indian educators today.	(Consider the early Carlisle; Haskell; Pembroke State; the new Navajo community college and their school at Rough Rock; the Indian school district at Rocky Boy, Montana; D-Q University; and the new Wyoming Indian High School.)
16. The terse or silent and humorless Indian of stereotype was exposed as	Irving, A Tour on the Prairies Deloria, "Indian Humor," Custer

an overgeneralized creation of white minds by Washington Irving. Irving found that the Indians he visited were as loquacious as Whites, and that they had a sense of humor which often came out in their storytelling and singing as well as in jokes they made or told. Indians are represented by intelligent and articulate spokesmen such as Ross Morres, Melvin Thom, Vine Deloria, Jr., Peter MacDonald, Vernon Bellecourt, and many others of genuine ability.	Died for Your Sins (Deloria provides a good sampling of Indian humor.) "Listen to His Many Voices," in Witt and Steiner's The Way White Horse Eagle, We Indians (White Horse Eagle's "story," which he managed to sell to his white European editor as "whole cloth," contains a number of tall tales. Indians helped to shape the American tradition of humor.)

D. Indians have had to adapt to a number
of forces which changed their modes of
life. In some cases adjustment was
welcomed; in others great difficulties
were involved.

1. Though captives were taken by raiding
parties, the captives often became
adopted members of the new tribe,
with equal rights with their captors.

2. There were policies which the
Spaniards and the Anglo Saxon Americans employed which precluded the
possibility of adaptation: work in

Johnson, A Man Called Horse
Berger, Little Big Man
Lowie, "A Crow Woman's Tale," in
Parsons' American Indian Life
(The theme of the white captive
of Indians has been almost incredibly popular in American
writings.)

the mercury mines was almost always fatal; "lead poisoning" at the hands of a frontiersman or a soldier was often incurable. The tribal organization was itself a remarkable strength to the Indian in withstanding or adapting to foreign culture.

3. The slaughter of the buffalo herds changed life for many Indians.

 a. After the buffalo were gone, white men brought cattle herds to graze. A number of Indians became cowboys and ranchers.

  (1) Though most tribes were not outstanding as livestock breeders, some, such as the Nez Percé and the Cayuse Indians, were noted for their fine herds of horses and cattle in the nineteenth century. Lewis and Clark compared the horses of these two tribes to those of Kentucky.

  (2) The Indians' superior horsemanship and knowledge of the country proved useful to them

McNickle, Native American Tribalism

Deloria, Custer Died for Your Sins (a really important statement on tribalism)

Collier, The Indians of the Americas

Capps, The White Man's Road (Treats the need of the Indian to make the transition to grazing cattle on their own lands.)

Cushman, Stay Away, Joe (Contains insights into the problems an Indian cattleman might face in becoming established.)

(The Appaloosa breed of today is descended from horses the Nez Percé Indians raised in the Palouse River country and which they used in the 1870's to outmaneuver the U.S. Cavalry, under the brilliant direction of Joseph, Looking Glass, and Ollicut.)

as cowboys and ranchers in the
West.

(3) A number of Indian cowboys were
legendary figures in their own
time. Sam Dunn, eldest son of
the first owner of the old 7U
Ranch in Owyhee County, Idaho,
described two Native American
cowboys from whom he learned
much of his own roping and
riding skill.

(4) A number of modern-day Indians
in the West still maintain their
cowboy skills. One may see
Native American participants in
rodeos wherever rodeos are held.

(5) Some Western tribes have made
good use of their grazing lands
(where they were fortunate
enough to have good grazing
lands on their reservations).

E. Indians have made remarkable contributions to the American way of life.

1. The manner in which Indian life
helped to maintain an ecological
balance is being studied to help

Borland, When the Legends Die
(The novel's hero is a rodeo
bronc rider.)
(Little Joe Bowers was best at
roping horses of all the cowboys
along the Nevada-Idaho line.
The greatest bronc rider Dunn
knew [and he grew up with J.
Hugo Strickland, one-time world
champion bronc rider] was a
Duckwater Indian.)
(Some rodeos such as the one at
Flagstaff's Powwow are sponsored
by Indians with all contestants
being Indians.)
(For example the San Carlos Apaches,
the Bannock-Shoshonis of Idaho,
and the Arapahoes and Shoshonis
of Wyoming, all have fine herds
which graze on productive ranges.)

modern America solve the crisis

situation in America's environment

today.

2. In every war that America has fought, there have been Indian heroes fighting beside Whites.

(In recent wars Native Americans have transmitted and received strategic messages in their own languages, which enemy forces did not understand.)

F. Individuals have demonstrated that there is no conceivable human activity in which it is impossible for Native Americans to excel, as this representative (though by no means complete) list shows.

- Leaders in Politics, Business: (including some offices they have held): Louis R. Bruce (Commissioner of Indian Affairs during part of the Nixon Administration); Harry Rainbolt (Executive Assistant Indian Affairs Commission, in Nixon Administration); Ely Parker (Union Brigadier General, General Grant's military secretary, Commissioner of Indian Affairs, 1869-1871, and later Wall Street millionaire); LaDonna Harris (organizer of Americans for Indian Opportunity); Thomas Segundo (Papago tribal leader); Ben Reifel (former U.S. Congressman from South Dakota); Alex Chasing Hawk (contemporary leader); Ross Morres (Director, Nevada Indian Affairs Commission); Melvin Thom (former president of NIYC, member of Walker River Paiute Tribal Council); Vernon L. Ashley (Chairman of Governors' Interstate Indian Council); Peter MacDonald (tribal chairman of the Navajo Nation); Raymond Nakai (former Navajo Tribal Council Chairman); Annie Dodge Wauneka (Navajo tribal leader); Jake Chee

(Navajo legislator); Robert Lewis (Zuni leader); Joseph R. Garry (tribal leader of Couer d'Alenes, legislator); W. W. Keeler (Cherokee leader, former board chairman of Phillips Petroleum); Earl Old Person (Chairman, Blackfeet Tribal Council, President of NCAI); Lehman Brightman, Dennis Banks, Carter Camp, Leonard Grow Dog, Mike Chosa, Russell Means, Wallace "Mad Bear" Anderson, Clyde Bellecourt and Vernon Bellecourt (contemporary leaders who have been associated with Red Power)

- Athletes:

Louis Bennett ("Deerfoot"--19th century Seneca distance runner who competed successfully on both sides of the Atlantic, even in his sixties); Louis Tewanima (Hopi distance runner, 2nd in 1912 Olympic 10,000 meters though he was then in his forties); Billy Mills (Sioux distance runner, winner of 1964 Olympic 10,000 meters); Ernie "Indian Red" Lopez (boxer); Tom Skenandore (first paid football player for Green Bay, in 1896); Jim Thorpe (Sac and Fox Olympic Champion, college and professional football great); Sonny Sixkiller (outstanding quarterback); Indian Joe Guyon (Chippewa college All American, Pro-Football Hall of Fame); Wahoo Sam Crawford and Allie Reynolds (great baseball stars)

- Education, Science, Law:

Eugene Sekaquaptewa (former director, Center for Indian Education at Arizona State University, now head of Hopi tribal education system); George Lee (College president, Navajo Community College); Dillon Platero (Director of the Navajo school at Roughrock, New Mexico); Tom Shakespeare (religious leader of Native American Church, Native American Studies director at Wyoming Indian High School); Alfonso Ortiz (Tewa anthropologist); Gabriel Horn (teacher and poet); Lloyd H. New (Director, Institute of

American Indian Arts); Will Antell (Minnesota Director of Indian Education); Ned Hatathli (Navajo Community College); Ralph A. Farrow (professor of education); John C. Rainer, Jr. (on faculty of Brigham Young University); Alonzo T. Spang (Navajo Community College); Montana Rickard (college professor); D'Arcy McNickle (professor of anthropology); Helen Redbird Salem (college professor); Wilford C. Wasson (professor of ethnic studies and anthropology); Robert L. Bennett (Director, American Indian Law Center, University of New Mexico); William J. Benham, Francis McKinley, Leonard Bearking, Mary Nelson, Deb J. Victor and George A. Gill (other noted Indian educators); Arnold T. Anderson (Iroquois business executive and scientist who was on the team which worked to develop atomic energy in World War II); Brantley Blue (Commissioner, Indian Court of Claims); Edward McGaa and Ramon Roubideaux (prominent Indian attorneys)

- Writers:

N. Scott Momaday (Pulitzer Prize novelist, poet, literary scholar); Vine Deloria, Jr. (brilliant essayist); D'Arcy McNickle (anthropologist and author); Simon Ortiz and James Welch (poets); Durango Mendoza, Rupert Weeks, Kay Bennett, Natachee Scott Momaday, D. Chief Eagle, Chiron Khanshendel, John Joseph Mathews, Gerald Robert Vizenor, Charles A. Eastman and Francis LaFlesche (other important Native American writers); LeRoi Smith (editorial director of TRM Publications); Allen P. Slickpoo, Sr.; Carolyn Wright (editor, Native Nevadan); Howard Rock (editor, Tundra Times); Rupert Costo, Henry Azbill, and Jeannette Henry (editors of Indian Historian Press publications); and Jake Herman (columnist and humorist in Indian Historian)

- The Arts, Entertainment:

  Jay Silverheels (film actor); Dan George (stage and film actor); Maria
  Tallchief (classic ballerina); Marjorie Tallchief (ballerina); Moscalyne
  Larkin (ballerina, choreographer, teacher); Louis Ballard (musician,
  composer, teacher); Marvin Rainwater (singer); Kay Starr (singer, enter-
  tainer); Buffy Sainte Marie (singer, songwriter); Arthur S. Junalaska
  (playwright, theatrical director); Maria Montoya Martinez and Tony Da
  (ceramicists); Acee Blue Eagle, Pablita Velarde, George Morrison, Beatien
  Yazz, Rafael Medina, Joe Merrera, Joan Hill, Oscar Howe, Teofilo Tafoya,
  Geronima Cruz Montoya, Robert Draper, Jose Aquilar, Harrison Begay,
  R. C. Gorman, Fritz Scholder, Popovi Da, Al Momaday, Matt Tashquinth
  and Ray Naha (artists).

III   Conclusion

Indians in what is now the United States shrank steadily in numbers from
the time Whites first appeared in America until the early twentieth century.
At present they are a rapidly increasing minority, having more than doubled
in numbers since the early part of this century.

There are problems which the Indian faces today. In general Indians have
worse health (or worse health care) than any other American ethnic group. The
average Indian lives forty-four years. Indians also complete fewer years of
schooling than other groups. And, like the Chicano, an Indian may grow up
speaking a language other than English.

The tribal cultures themselves are amazingly rich and enduring. Tribal
Indian cultures have made important contributions to American life. America's
most valuable agricultural crop, corn, is a product of Indian agriculture.
And ideals of American democracy were drawn from Indian models.

In America's history Indians have produced men as brave and devoted as
Crazy Horse, as humane and far-sighted as Tecumseh, as linguistically inventive
as Sequoyah, as physically capable as Jim Thorpe, as statesmanlike as John Ross,
as articulate as Vine Deloria, and as artistically expressive as N. Scott
Momaday, Simon Ortiz and Maria Tallchief. America has need of such people and
of the culture which can produce them. It is time that America should stop
whitewashing its red men.

GLOSSARY

The following short glossary may be helpful. As American Indian languages are many, only a few terms are listed here, some from various Indian languages, some of English, French, and Spanish origin.

Acequia: A Spanish word; a canal used for irrigation by Indians of the Southwest such as Navajos and Pueblos

Allotment: A division of the tribal reservation resulting from pressures brought to "Americanize" Indians by breaking up communally owned and operated reservations into parcels owned by individuals

Agency Indian: An Indian who accepted the protection of the U.S. Government and who settled near a federal outpost or agency; antonyms were "wild Indians," or "hostiles"

Appaloosa: A breed of horse developed by the Nez Perce Indians

Apple: A descriptive metaphor applied to an Indian who is "red on the outside, white on the inside"; one who has "sold out" or who represents or promotes non-Indian ideals; an Uncle Tomahawk

Blanket: An item of trade; those made by skilled weavers of the Southwest serving several purposes, including use as wearing apparel; the term "blanket Indian" meant one who maintained traditional Indian ways

Boarding School: A school usually operated by the Bureau of Indian Affairs at which young Indian students lived and studied

Bosque Redondo: A reservation and "reformatory" in New Mexico Territory where Navajos and some Apaches were exiled in the 1860's

Buck: A term usually carrying an unfavorable connotation, denoting an Indian (or sometimes a black) male

Bureau of Indian Affairs (BIA): The arm of the federal government which administers government Indian programs, now a part of the Interior Department but once part of the War Department

Cacique: A Spanish word used in the Southwest among the Pueblos and others to mean chief or leader of a community

Calumet: A word of French derivation; a long stemmed tobacco pipe; peace pipe

Chief: A title of leadership; as Indians usually exercised much less coercive forms of leadership than Whites, the significance of the title is often misinterpreted in writings about Indians; a nickname given to many Indians by their white colleagues or acquaintances

26

Cradleboard: A device employed by some Indian tribes in transporting and
    caring for infants

Fish In: Demonstrations, mainly in the Northwest and in other areas where
    fishing is an important source of livelihood, to protest the viola-
    tion of treaties by state governments

Five Civilized Tribes: The great Indian nations of the Southeast, Cherokees,
    Chickasaws, Choctaws, Creeks and Seminoles

Friendly/Hostile: Opposing terms or antonyms; friendlies were sympathetic
    to the U.S. Government or at least not in open opposition to it, while
    hostiles were adamant in refusing to give up their Indian ways and terri-
    tory; opposition between friendlies and hostiles sometimes became open
    conflict as in the case of the Hopis in 1906

Head Chief: A title usually bestowed upon an Indian appointed by the U.S.
    Government; with some exceptions, Indians did not ordinarily have al-
    liances of tribes which appointed or elected a head chief; usually each
    tribe had its own leader who rose to leadership and remained there
    through his own ability, not through heredity or outside manipulation

Heirship: A legal problem which arose as a result of making individual allot-
    ments, often making land of individual owners inaccessible or unusable
    to their heirs

Hogan: A Navajo dwelling

Indian Claims Commission: A federal provision of legal means for compensation
    to Indian tribes for loss of lands, established in 1946

Indian Princess: A title devised by white men; as there was no hereditary
    royalty among Indians in North America, there were no titles such as
    "princess"

Kachina: Hopi and Pueblo messengers from the gods, impersonated by priests
    in masks and costumes in religious ceremonials

Kiva: Hopi or Pueblo ceremonial chamber, mainly subterranean

La Crosse: A word of French origin; a ball game first played by North American
    Indians

League of the Iroquois: The powerful confederation of tribes of the Northeast
    which dated from the time of Hiawatha, the laws and agreements by which
    the Iroquois governed themselves

Lodge: The dwelling of an Indian; a tipi, wickiup or other similar structure

Longhair: An Indian who lives in the traditional Indian way, rejecting white
    culture

Longhouse: Communal swelling of the Iroquois

The Long Walk: The return of the Navajos to their homeland in 1868 after five years of exile at Bosque Redondo

Massacre: In traditional usage in relation to the Indians, the word massacre usually meant an Indian victory, for example "The Fetterman Massacre"

Medicine Man: A holy man among the Indians; a shaman; one who practiced the healing arts and who was entrusted with sacred objects and rituals

Metate: From the Nahuatl; a stone with a concave upper surface, used by Indians of the Southwest in grinding corn and other seeds

Native American Church: An Indian religion based in part on traditional Indian religious beliefs and in part on Christianity; one aspect of the ceremonials is the use of peyote

Naturalization: The process by which, under a 1940 Congressional provision, Indians could become U.S. citizens

Old Oraibi: A Hopi community in Arizona; the oldest continuously inhabited settlement in the United States

Pan Indianism: A movement to involve all Indians beyond tribal lines, to promote the common interests of Indian peoples

Papoose: A Narraganset word; a young child of North American Indian parents

Pemmican: A Cree word; dried lean meat mixed with fat and pounded to a paste, preserved in pressed cakes; recipes often include berries

Peonage: In the Southwest, a mild form of slavery in which Indians (Navajos and Apaches were the most popular) or Mexicans were captured or otherwise reduced to a lifetime of servitude

The People: Some Indian groups had a word for themselves which might translate as "the people" or "human beings"; others, including Anglo Americans and Indians not of the group, were not considered people or human beings

Piki: Paper thin bread made from fine cornflour, a forerunner to corn flakes

Piki Stone: A carefully selected, shaped and prepared stone on which Piki is cooked

Powwow: A word of Algonquian origin; a priest or medicine man; a conference or assembly of Indians, often with ceremonies, feasting and dancing

Pueblo: A communal village of some Indians of the Southwest, such as the Hopis, Zunis, and Pueblos

Rancheria: A small Indian settlement or collection of ranchos in the Southwest

Relocation: A federal policy designed to move Indians off reservations

Reservation: Territory set aside for a particular Indian group or groups and secured to them by treaty

Ricos: A Spanish word in common use throughout the Southwest; Navajo and other owners of herds and other wealth

Sachem: An Algonquian word denoting the supreme chief of a confederation of Algonquian tribes; any North American Indian chief

Sand Painting: The practice of Navajo and Hopi artistry using colored sand; the paintings have a religious significance and among the Hopi are regarded as being sacred in such a way that they are always carefully erased and never preserved

Savage: A term used traditionally by Whites to designate Indians; use of the word was often coupled with the word "heathen"

Sign Language: A widely used North American Indian system of communication employing gestures

Squaw: An Algonquian word for woman or wife; often used by Whites in derogation

Squaw Man: A word bearing a negative connotation, attached to a white man who had taken an Indian wife

Sun Dance: A religious ceremony of the Plains Indians; outlawed for a time because of its "pagan" nature

Succotash: A word of Narraganset origin; a dish consisting of beans and corn cooked together

Termination: A Hoover Commission recommendation of 1949 adopted by Congress as a federal policy in 1953; its purpose was to terminate federal trusteeship and responsibility to Indian tribes

Tipi: Conical dwelling of Plains Indians, made of buffalo skins, with lodgepoles for support

Tomahawk: An Algonquian word for a light ax, originally with a bone or stone head, used as a tool or weapon

Trail of Tears: The journey of the Cherokees and others from their homes in the Southeast to Indian Territory, in which great numbers died of the hardships imposed on them

Treaty: An agreement between the U.S. Government and an Indian tribe or tribes, the usual purpose of which was to obtain Indian lands for white settlement

Tribalism: The Indian communal cultural way of life

Wakontankan: The Great Spirit or supreme deity of the Sioux and their
    associates

Wampum: Beads used as money or pledges or as ornaments; wampum belts and
    strings of the Iroquois recorded important historical events and
    treaties

Wasichu, White Eyes, Long Knives: Some of the terms used by Indians to
    designate white men

Water Rights: A crucial contemporary issue; Indians' rights to water are
    being challenged today as their rights to land were challenged a
    century ago

Wheeler Howard Act (Indian Reorganization Act): Enacted during the Roosevelt
    Administration, the act allowed tribes to incorporate with their own
    charters and constitutions and to plan their own development

Wickiup: Conical dwellings of Indians such as the Fox tribe, made of bark,
    rushes, grass, sod, with poles for support

PART TWO: INDIANS IN CONFLICT

I   Introduction

The American Indian's history is characterized by struggle. Though he
lived in relative harmony with his environment, his relationship with nature
was marked by conflict as well. Wresting a living from the woods, mountains,
plains, and streams required skill in stalking game or in growing crops or
gathering sufficient for his needs. Recurring cycles of scant rain brought
hardship to the Southwest Indian. Migrations of the buffalo left the Plains
Indian without his main source of sustenance, until, with acquisition of the
horse, he was able to cover vast distances himself as he followed the wild
herds.

The Indian was involved in continual intertribal warfare. For many of
America's Indian tribes, training for warfare was an integral part of a young
man's educational background. Skill in use of weapons was important to him,
as was fleetness of foot or horsemanship.

Though there were cultural conflicts which developed as European immi-
grants settled America, the most important conflict which the Indian was to
face was over the land itself. The first European settlers were cautious,
perhaps a little humble, in their suit for Indian lands. But as Whites in-
creased in numbers, their pleas became demands. "Manifest destiny" and,
later, social Darwinism provided logical excuses for raw capitalism, for race
war, and even provided a justification for genocide, as Whites plundered the
indigenous American. The Indian resisted American imperialism, but sheer
strength of numbers and technology of war were against him.

II   Guide and Sourcebook

Study Outline	*Notes and Sources*
A. Indians faced a number of natural or environmental conflicts.	
1. The problem of **gathering, or hunting,** or **growing** food was more or less acute from tribe to tribe.	Wheat, <u>The Survival Arts of the Primitive Paiutes</u> Lurie, <u>Mountain Wolf Woman</u>
2. Ecological changes often wrought disaster among the tribes. The loss of the buffalo reduced the Plains	O'Kane, <u>Sun in the Sky</u> Kroeber and Heizer, <u>Almost Ancestors</u>

31

Study Outline	*Notes and Sources*
Indians to poverty and dependency they had not before experienced. Many small tribes of California Indians became extinct as delicate ecological systems were disrupted at the coming of the Spanish, and radically altered at the coming of the Anglo Americans.	Kroeber, Ishi in Two Worlds

3. Diseases new to Indians decimated their ranks.

   a. When Squanto returned to his home in America before the Pilgrims landed, none of his people remained alive.

   b. Smallpox took a terrible toll. In the Southwest the Pueblos were drastically reduced in strength by a smallpox epidemic long before Anglo-Americans arrived on the scene. And the dread disease ravaged tribe after tribe.

Guthrie, The Big Sky (In the novel, most of Teal Eye's tribe die in a smallpox epidemic.) (The village dwelling Mandans and the powerful Blackfeet were reduced to a fraction of their former numbers.)

   c. White officials, guilty of criminal neglect, allowed disease to spread. General Hugh L. Scott opposed the nomination of R. V. Belt as Commissioner of Indian Affairs during

(See the Kiowa story "Saynday and Smallpox" in Marriott and Rachlin's American Indian Mythology.)

Study Outline	Notes and Sources
Cleveland's presidency, recounting Belt's actions when children of the Kiowa school were stricken with measles.	(Scott said of Belt: "Instead of keeping them quarantined...he turned them all out carrying the infection to every family, and, shortly after brought the Comanches as well as the Kiowas into camp...with the consequence that the Kiowas lost three hundred children in one month.")

4. Left to work out by themselves the problems of dealing with nature, the Indians developed practical and usually well balanced systems which sustained their own lives and the balance of nature.

(A relatively constant state of warfare helped keep the human population in check. Hunting and gathering modes of life served to keep the population fairly well distributed most of the time.)

B. The Indians lived in a state of more or less constant warfare among themselves: traditional rivalries existed over long periods of time, but alliances and enmities shifted from time to time.

Deloria, Custer Died for Your Sins (Indians distrusted each other as much as they distrusted Whites. Whites capitalized on Indian enmities in their imperialistic expansion.)

Josephy, The Patriot Chiefs

1. Massassoit found the Pilgrims to be of aid to him in his battles against neighboring tribes.

2. Mohegans and Pequots, traditional enemies of the Wampanoags, helped to bring about Philip's defeat.

3. The powerful Iroquois confederation of the North were opposed by the Cherokees in the South.

4. Creeks and Cherokees were enemies,
    and both tribes opposed the
    Seminoles.

5. The Cheyennes were generally on good   Grinnell, <u>The Fighting Cheyennes</u>
    terms with the Arapahoes and were   Plenty-Coups, "Those Who Made
    allied with the Sioux in most of the   War Against the White Man Always
    United States wars against Plains   Failed," in Witt and Steiner's
    Indians. Cheyennes were long at war   <u>The Way</u>
    with Utes, Pawnees, Shoshonis, and   Parsons, <u>American Indian Life</u>
    the Assiniboins. Later they were at   (especially the first two
    war with the Kiowas, Comanches and   "stories")
    Crows. Their last major war with
    Kiowas, Comanches and Apaches was
    fought in 1838.

6. One reason that the flight of the Nez   Garcia, <u>Tough Trip Through</u>
    Percés in 1877 stretched over such a   <u>Paradise</u> (Even so, they were
    long and twisting route was their   harassed and killed by Indians
    desire to avoid their Indian enemies.   as well as Whites.)

7. Apaches and Navajos staged raids on   Spicer, <u>Cycles of Conquest</u>
    Pueblos and Hopis over a period of   Waters, <u>Book of the Hopi</u>
    centuries. Pueblo and Hopi villages   Lauritzen, <u>Arrows into the Sun</u>
    were built as citadels to withstand   (This novel bears in part on
    just such attacks. Navajos and Utes   the Navajo-Ute rivalry.)
    were also at war with each other.   Bailey, <u>The Indian Slave-Trade</u>
    And these powerful tribes also raided   <u>in the Southwest</u>

the Paiutes to take their women and

children for slaves.

C. There were race wars between Whites and

Indians, usually over land.

1. In Virginia

    a. In 1585 Sir Richard Grenville   Collier, The Indians of the

        landed in what is now Virginia,   Americas (One of his hosts stole

        exploring as far as the present   from him a small silver cup; in

        Roanoke River and finding hospit-   return, Grenville sacked and

        able Indians.   burned the Indian's village.)

    b. The white settlement at Jamestown   (After Powhatan [Waukunsenecaw]

        was not bothered by the Powhatans,   died in 1622, his successor,

        although they could easily have   Opechancanough, attempted to

        destroyed it.   destroy the white colony and

2. In New England   failed, for by that time the

    a. Coastal explorers and traders who   balance of power had shifted.)

        preceded the Pilgrims had been re-   Josephy, The Patriot Chiefs

        ceived with curiosity and kindness   (Squanto was one of the 24.

        by native Americans until 1614,   Taken to London, he learned the

        when Thomas Hunt kidnapped 24 of   customs and language of the

        them and sold them as slaves in   British before shipping back to

        Malaga. Kindly monks ransomed some   America in 1619.)

        of these and gave them their free-

        dom.

    b. In March of 1621, Samoset, who had   (Massassoit was to be a valuable

        learned English from traders, came   friend to the Whites throughout

Study Outline	_Notes and Sources_

to greet the Pilgrims and to offer his friendship. Soon afterward, Samoset brought Squanto, Massassoit and sixty Wampanoag men to visit the Pilgrims.

his life, rendering them aid and ceding them land. Squanto taught them to raise crops **for** food.)

c. In 1637 Puritans drove the Pequots from harbors in the Long Island Sound which the Puritans had found desirable. The Dutch were also participants in this war against the Pequots. John Mason led a night attack, burning the Pequot village and shooting the Indians by light of the flames.

Cotton Mather, excerpts from Narratives of the Indian Wars, in Anderson and Wright's The Dark and Tangled Path (Cotton Mather wrote of the massacre: "It was supposed that no less than six hundred Pequot souls were brought down to hell that day.")

d. In 1675 and 1676 King Philip's War was fought. Philip, Massassoit's son, gained the help of a number of Indian tribes to wage war against the Whites.

(1) Philip's object was to sweep the Whites off the continent.

(2) Several factors were in Philip's disfavor: the Indians were not accustomed to the sustained warfare which he knew was necessary to accomplish his purpose; the

(Indian warfare seemed brutal and strange to the colonists, but the colonists were quick to adopt Indian savagery to add to their own forms of brutality.)

(Of the 90 white settlements in New England, 52 were attacked and 12 completely destroyed in the war.)

Josephy, "The Betrayal of King Philip," The Patriot Chiefs (Perhaps the most important of these factors was the aid the

Study Outline	Notes and Sources

constancy of some of the allied tribes was often in question; and there were traditional enemies of the Wampanoags (the Mohegans and Pequots) who joined the Praying Indians (Christian converts) in assisting the Whites.

Whites received from other Indians, which had the effect of turning the tide of battle against Philip.)

e. In the French and Indian War, many of the Indians aligned themselves with the French. But Quakers succeeded in binding members of the Iroquois Confederacy to themselves and to England, bringing a balance of power to the English side.

Pontiac, "It Is Hard to Fight Among Brethren for the Sake of Dogs," in Witt and Steiner's The Way (Indians were often the deciding factor in wars of the colonial period.)

3. Pontiac's War

a. In Pontiac's war against the British colonists, Pontiac captured eight of the twelve British forts in Indian country, forced another to be abandoned, and laid prolonged sieges on Fort Detroit and Fort Pitt.

b. Two of the factors which had contributed to the outbreak were that

(During the war Amherst suggested extermination of the Indians:

Study Outline	Notes and Sources
British traders, who had replaced the French after the French and Indian War, were much less generous than the French had been; and, General Jeffrey Amherst, who commanded the troops, was extremely rigid and prejudicial in his dealings with the Indians. When Amherst returned to England, Pontiac still had the upper hand, though he could see that his course was not to succeed.	You will do well to try to innoculate the Indians by means of blankets which smallpox patients have slept, as well as by other means that can serve to extirpate this execrable race.) (With the defeat of the Indians in the Pontiac War, white settlers began moving west of the mountains.)

4. The Shawnee Wars and Indian Federation.

    a. In 1774 in Lord Dunmore's War between the Shawnees and Virginia colonists, Cornstalk, the Shawnee leader, was forced to surrender Shawnee claims to lands south of the Ohio River, allowing Virginians to open Kentucky to settlement.

(Whites did not keep their pledge to remain south of the Ohio. A band of white frontiersmen shot Puckeshinwa, Tecumseh's father, in the Shawnee woods, and left him to die.)

    b. Cornstalk, Tecumseh's hero, was killed by a mob of soldiers when he made a peaceful visit to the American fort at Point Pleasant.

Study Outline	Notes and Sources

c. Blackfish, Cornstalk's successor, commenced a war of revenge. In 1778, he led his people in an invasion of Kentucky.

(Blackfish captured Daniel Boone [who later escaped] and 26 other Whites in the 1778 campaign. This border war was a peripheral part of the Revolution.)

d. In 1780 George Rogers Clark led an American army which drove the Shawnees from their settlements in Old Chillicothe and Old Piqua.

(Clark burned the two cities.)

e. In 1790 General Josiah Harmer, who had been ordered to give protection to Whites in the Northwest Territory, marched into the Ohio and Indiana countries of the Shawnees at the head of 1400 men, determined to teach the natives a lesson.

Porter, Battle of the 1,000 Slain (Chapter 2) (Little Turtle, a Miami war chief, appealed to all Indians to join him at the site of presentday Fort Wayne. Tecumseh and others joined Little Turtle to defeat Harmer.)

f. Other expeditions continued to harass the Indians. In 1791 General Arthur St. Clair led more than 2000 men against the Indians.

(Under Little Turtle's leadership, the Indians destroyed St. Clair's army, killing more than 600 and sending the survivors back across the Ohio. The flow of settlers to the Northwest Territory was halted for a time.)

g. In 1794 Blue Jacket and Tecumseh with 1400 men met Anthony Wayne and his 3000 at the battle of Fallen Timbers. Victorious, Wayne proceeded to destroy every Indian village in the vicinity and built Fort Wayne. The following spring,

(Tecumseh refused to attend the signing of the treaty and later refused to accept what the chiefs had done. Disgruntled warriors

Study Outline	*Notes and Sources*

representatives of twelve tribes were reluctant signers of the Greenville Treaty, ceding much Indian land in the Northwest Territory.

(joined him, giving their loyalty and making him the dominant leader in the Northwest.)

h. In Tecumseh's campaign to unite Indians everywhere, he failed to secure support of the Iroquois League. Meeting a mixed response elsewhere, with some whole tribes favoring alliance and some opposing, Tecumseh gained the support of the Ottowa chief, Shabbona, and the Sauk and Fox war leader, Black Hawk.

(Tecumseh was joined by his brother Laulwasika [later known as Tenskwatawa the Prophet] who had renounced liquor and the white man's influence after having become a drunkard.)

Tecumseh, "Will We Let Ourselves Be Destroyed?" in Witt and Steiner's The Way

i. In 1809, after "mellowing" Indian leaders with alcohol, Governor Harrison obtained a cession of 3,000,000 acres of land, much of it owned by tribes not present at the Fort Wayne meeting, for $7000 in cash and an annuity of $1750.

(Tecumseh learned of the cession of much of the Shawnee land when he returned from meeting with New York Indian leaders.)

j. In 1811, during Tecumseh's absence, Harrison struck at the Prophet's Town at the mouth of the Tippecanoe

(Estimated Indian losses were between 25 and 40 men. Harrison lost 61 killed and 127 wounded.

Study Outline	*Notes and Sources*

with an army of almost 1000 men. Harrison drove the Indians out of their settlement which he then proceeded to destroy, firing all the buildings and stores of food.

Harrison wrote to the Secretary of War that "the Indians have never sustained so severe a defeat since their acquaintance with white people.")

5. The War of 1812.

   a. Tecumseh and his federation joined the British in the War of 1812. Tecumseh formed a winning leadership team with Canadian General Isaac Brock.

   (Tecumseh and Brock defeated General William Hull and his troops at Detroit.)

   b. Under Tecumseh's leadership, the British and Indians laid siege on Fort Meigs, which Harrison had just built and was occupying in 1813. Due to the vacillating leadership of Proctor, the seige was lifted.

   (A brigade of 1100 Kentucky riflemen who were coming to Harrison's assistance were soundly defeated by Tecumseh's Indians.)

   c. The British and Indians suddenly found themselves in a worse position when Perry swept the British from Lake Erie.

   d. Harrison, with a force of 3500 men, was able to defeat a retreating force of 700 British troops and Tecumseh's 1000 Indians.

   (Tecumseh himself was killed in the battle.)

Study Outline	*Notes and Sources*
e. On August 30, 1813, the "Red Stick" Upper Creeks attacked Fort Mims, in Alabama, killing 367 people.	(As the War of 1812 began, Tecumseh had visited the Creeks and Tallassees in Alabama, calling on them to join in a general war against the U.S. Those who were favorable to his plan he gave a calendar device of red sticks to coordinate the day of the first general attack.)
f. Andrew Jackson, aided by Cherokees, led an army of several thousand Tennessee militia, virtually wiping out the force of some 1000 "Red Stick" Creeks.	
g. The few surviving "Red Stick" Creeks and the Tallassees went south into Florida, which then belonged to Spain.	Red Eagle, "Your People Have Destroyed My Nation," in Witt and Steiner's The Way (As punishment for the hostilities of their relatives, the "White Stick" Creeks [who had not agreed to Tecumseh's plan and who had aided Jackson] were forced to sign a treaty ceding 8,000,000 acres [about two-thirds of the entire Creek land] to the U.S.)
6. The last of the Midwest/Northwest Wars.	
a. The Black Hawk War, last to be fought in the Northwest Territory, was precipitated by incidents which followed the 1803 Louisiana Purchase. Some Sauk Indians quarreled and fought with white settlers near St. Louis, killing three settlers in self-defense.	Josephy, "The Rivalry of Black Hawk and Keokuk," The Patriot Chiefs
b. Governor William Henry Harrison of Indiana Territory requested a meeting of Sauk chiefs and a surrender of the "murderers." The	(Harrison managed to get the Indians to make their marks on a treaty that ceded all their lands

Study Outline	Notes and Sources

Sauk and Foxes sent five men, including one who had been involved, to make suitable payment to secure release of the prisoner. Harrison refused to let the man go without a cession of Indian land.

c. Increasing pressure for removal came. White settlers moved onto Black Hawk's farmlands.

d. In 1831 General Gaines began his campaign against the uncooperative Black Hawk.

e. General Henry Atkinson mustered 1500 men for action against Black Hawk, while Black Hawk's numbers diminished to the point that he had only fifty or so with him at the moment he was attacked by Major Isaiah Stillman's force of 275 troops. Black Hawk and his men turned the attacking militia into a fleeing mob.

f. Black Hawk tried to surrender to the captain of the steamboat <u>Warrior</u> on the Mississippi. Black

east of the Mississippi. [The Indians claimed they were kept drunk.] Harrison then applied to President Jefferson for a pardon for the prisoner, but before it came the prisoner was killed in an escape attempt.)

(Federal support meanwhile had been given to Keokuk, who was willing to cooperate, creating a division among the Sauk and Foxes.)

(Black Hawk died in 1838. His grave was robbed and his bones placed on display in an Iowa museum. Keokuk died in 1848 in Kansas, where he had moved after selling the Sauk and Fox lands in Iowa. A bronze bust of Keokuk was placed in the Capitol in Washington, and he was hailed as "in every sense of the word a great man.")

Hawk's message was misunderstood by
the interpreter on the Warrior, and
the boat's six-pounder opened fire
at short range, killing 23 Indians.

g. Atkinson with a troop of 1300 engaged most of the Indians who were
trying to cross the Mississippi.
(Black Hawk and a few of his warriors were elsewhere.) The Americans clubbed and shot every Indian
they saw, including the women and
children.

7. The Seminole War.

a. In 1817 General Edmund P. Gaines
sent 250 men across the Florida
line to arrest a Seminole chief
who was charged with harboring escaped slaves. At Fowltown, the
chief's village, five Indians were
killed.

b. Late in November of 1817, Seminoles
assaulted a party of American soldiers in retaliation for the
Fowltown assault.

(The arrival of the Warrior en-
abled Atkinson to finish off some
of the Indians who were on islands.
And the Sioux, who were waiting
on the west bank of the river,
killed and scalped 68 and took
the rest of Black Hawk's people
prisoner. Whites took 39 prisoners
and counted 150 Indian bodies.)

(Andrew Jackson wrote to President
Monroe to:

"let it be signified to me
through any channel that the
possession of the Floridas
would be desirable to the
United States, and in sixty
days it will be accomplished.")

Van Every, Disinherited

44

Study Outline	*Notes and Sources*

c. Jackson and Gaines were then ordered to march across the Florida line if the Indians refused to make reparations. Jackson invaded with 2000 troops. The Lower Creeks (the "White Sticks") again helped Jackson, who burned Seminole villages and dispersed Indians he found.

d. Jackson became the first territorial governor of Florida. In 1823 commissioners gathered village chiefs to sign the Camp Moultrie Treaty restricting them to a reservation in the interior of Florida.

e. Difficulties arose. Reservation lands were unproductive; some Indians starved. Those who left the reservation were threatened. Slavehunters were encouraged to look in the Seminole villages for runaways.

f. In 1832, perhaps by craft or trickery, a number of Seminole leaders were talked into signing

Porter, <u>Battle of the 1,000 Slain</u> (Chapter 5) (Jackson's Florida campaign was directed against the Spanish as well as the Seminoles. Jackson moved his men through Florida, capturing the cities of St. Marks and Pensacola from the Spaniards, whom he blamed for having failed to keep the Indians in line. In 1819 Spain ceded Florida to the U.S.)

(The slavehunters claimed Negroes who were property of the Seminoles or who were actually members of the Seminole tribes, either born or adopted to freedom. Resentment arose; quarrels and conflicts broke out. Invading gangs of white men began shooting at Indians and the Seminoles retaliated.)

Study Outline	Notes and Sources

the Treaty of Payne's Landing which
conveyed their lands in Florida to
the United States and called for
the removal of the Indians to the
West.

g. The Florida Indians requested that
if they were to accept removal,
they be given their own government
agent and lands separate from the
Creeks who were their enemies.
Washington denied these requests.

h. The second Seminole War resulted.
In the war, Micanopy and Osceola
led their men in successful hit and
run raids.

i. Perhaps the most notable single
day's endeavor occurred when
Osceola led a group of men on a
daring raid on the reservation
headquarters, killing Agent Wiley
Thompson (who had put Osceola in
irons) and four other Whites. At
the same time, Micanopy, Jumper,
and Alligator led a larger group in
an ambush of two companies of ·

(Micanopy, leading chief of the
Seminoles; Jumper, one of the
"Red Stick" Creek leaders;
Osceola; and other leaders refused to sign a new removal
document after they had called
the Treaty of Payne's Landing
a forgery and had refused to abide
by it. Micanopy did not come to
sign. And upon Osceola's refusal,
he was placed in irons until he
agreed to sign.)

(The massacre of Dade's men
brought sterner measures from
President Jackson. In February
of 1836 General Edmund P. Gaines
was sent to Florida with a force
of about 1000 men, with Major
General Winfield Scott assuming
over-all command of the Florida
troops. Gaines and Scott were
both ineffectual against the

troops under Major Francis L. Dade. Only three soldiers of the 102 managed to return to Fort Brooke, and those three died of their wounds.

j. In the fall of 1836 Gen. Thomas S. Jesup became American commander of the Florida campaign army which was raised in strength to 8000 men.

k. Osceola's Indians resting in camps awaiting removal learned that slave catchers were circulating among Micanopy's people claiming both Indians and Negroes, with Jesup providing no protection to the Seminoles.

l. Some Seminoles managed to hold out until the U.S. troops left. The main resistance ended when Osceola, then too ill to walk, was put in chains and imprisoned with his party of about 100, when he met with military leader Joseph M. Hernandez under a flag of truce.

Indians. After two months, Scott was transferred to Alabama to fight the Creeks.)

(In 1837 Jesup's army was able to coerce Micanopy and other leaders into signing an agreement to emigrate peacefully.)

(Osceola and other chiefs at Ft. Mellon obtained permission to visit their villages and then return. Instead of returning, Osceola and some 200 men surrounded the camps of Micanopy and Jumper, taking the two chiefs with them. Hostilities were resumed.)

(Osceola, suffering from malaria and near the point of death with an attack of quinsy, refused treatment at the hands of Dr. Frederick Weedon, the post surgeon, a brother-in-law of Indian agent Wiley Thompson. After

Study Outline	Notes and Sources
m. The United States lost 1500 lives and $20,000,000 in the futile attempt to remove all the Florida Indians. Seminoles live in the Florida Everglades today.	Osceola's death, Dr. Weedon cut off the chief's head and kept it as a souvenir.)
8. The 1830's and Choctaw Removal	(Thomas Jefferson had said in 1786:
a. Prior to the War of 1812, Indians had been forced by the government to sign treaties to give some semblance of legality to white acquisition of Indian lands.	"It may be regarded as certain that not a foot of land will ever be taken from the Indians without their consent. The sacredness of their rights is felt by all thinking persons in America as much as in Europe.")
b. In the expansionist period that followed the War of 1812, there was little regard for even the outward forms of legality as settlers began to encroach upon the territory of the Cherokees, Creeks, Chickasaws, Choctaws and Seminoles. Indian tribes were ordered to get out or be driven out by troops.	
c. Following Jackson's signing of the Indian Removal Bill in May of 1830, there was a concerted attempt to move the Five Civilized Tribes west.	(The Indian Removal Bill made provision for trading tribal lands for territory west of the Mississippi and for mandatory removal of Indians to the West.)

Study Outline	Notes and Sources

d. Four of the tribes were asked to
    send representatives to meet with
    President Jackson and Secretary of
    War John H. Eaton. Only the
    Chickasaws appeared.

e. Jackson refused to make any con-   (The U.S. Senate refused to
    cessions to the Chickasaws, so they   ratify this agreement.)
    reluctantly signed an agreement
    to migrate, on the conditions that
    they be reimbursed for their lands
    east of the Mississippi and that
    the proposed western location be
    suitable.

f. Taking a new tack, the administra-   (Federal commissioners were aided
    tion increased pressures to gain   by an act of the Mississippi
    general consent of the Indians to   legislature which provided fines
    migrate. The Choctaw nation was   and imprisonment for any Indian
    chosen to serve as a positive ex-   who attempted to direct, advise
    ample for the other tribes, proving   or influence other Indians.)
    that such an action could be ac-
    complished smoothly.

g. Generals John H. Eaton and John   (Following the signing of the
    Coffee offered bribes of money and   Treaty of Dancing Rabbit Creek,
    public rewards of Mississippi land   Whites swarmed onto Indian lands.
    to a number of representatives of   Indians who left their homes
    the Choctaws in exchange for   even for a few hours returned to

signing the Treaty of Dancing Rabbit Creek in September of 1830. The treaty then had the appearance of legality. The Senate ratified it.

h. From the fall of 1831 to the spring of 1832, the migration of some 13,000 Choctaws was directed by the Army. The migration itself had appeared simple to Whites--so simple that very little planning was done. Money had been appropriated but the contractors aiding removal made delays to lengthen the time in which supplies had to be furnished and withheld food deliveries until they were able to get what monies the Indians themselves had.

i. Of the 7000 who had not yet joined the migrants, most refused to leave Mississippi, becoming sharecroppers on the land they had owned.

find them looted. Whites also peddled liquor to the demoralized Choctaws. Swindles became common.)

(The whole enterprise was a fiasco, with groups of Indians being abandoned in the wilderness without food or shelter, with delays at river crossings and with landings at inappropriate locations. The winter of migration was the worst in memory. To add a final touch, the region of lower Mississippi through which they had to travel was the scene of a cholera epidemic. Crowded in unsanitary camps and under the stress of moving, the Choctaws died by hundreds. The aim for a "good example" for other Indians to follow had missed its mark. The other tribes were horrified by the prospect that faced them in removal.)

9. The Trail of Tears

    a. John Ross's Cherokee policy of

        non-violence and appeal to reason

        in dealing with the United States

        brought support from New England

        and from a number of white leaders,

        including Henry Clay, Daniel

        Webster, Edward Everett, John

        Howard Payne, Sam Houston and Davy

        Crockett.

    b. But the insatiable demand for more

        land for the slave-plantation South

        was not to be denied.

        (1) Georgians, led by Governor

             Lumpkin, were quick to point

             out that all the other states

             had been ceded large tracts of

             Indian lands when Georgia had

             not been so favored.

        (2) Georgia's anti-Cherokee omnibus

             act, which had been passed in

             1829, to take effect in 1830,

             was an aid to removal. Presi-

             dent Jackson, of course, was

             eager to help remove the Chero-

             kees, despite their appeals to

Van Every, Disinherited

(Ralph Waldo Emerson spoke to
the moral issue of Cherokee removal
in a letter to President Van Buren:

"...how could we call a conspiracy that should crush these
poor Indians our government, or
the land that was cursed by
their parting and dying impre-
cations our country, any more?
You, sir, will bring down that
renowned chair in which you sit
into infamy if your seal is set
to this instrument of perfidy;
and the name of this nation,
hitherto the sweet omen of religion and liberty, will stink
to the world.")

(Some provisions of the omnibus

act:

confiscation by the state of
Cherokee land (to be distributed
to white settlers by lottery);

abolition of Cherokee government
and nullification of all Cherokee
law;

prohibition of all meetings of
Cherokees (including religious
meetings as well as councils);

him as former allies against the Creeks.

(3) President Jackson did not want to interfere with states' rights by any move against the omnibus bill.

c. "Divide and conquer" tactics were used. A few wealthy Cherokee leaders were promised their lands and possessions in exchange for support for removal of the others.

d. Harassment became policy. Ross was abducted by Georgia officials while he was in Tennessee. John Howard Payne had been with Ross when he was taken and was his fellow captive. The incident created a sensation when Payne publicized what had happened.

e. Attorney William Wirt brought a Cherokee case against the state of Georgia to the Supreme Court. The Court's 1831 decision was no aid to the Cherokee cause.

f. A later case involved Samuel Worcester, a missionary to the

imprisonment of Cherokees who advised other Cherokees not to accept removal;

denial of the right of any Cherokee to testify in court against a White;

abrogation of all contracts between Indians and Whites unless witnessed by two Whites;

denial of Cherokee right to dig for gold in the recently discovered Cherokee gold fields.)

(The factionalism which resulted was to cost Ross and his group the support of Edward Everett and some others who had been staunch defenders of Cherokee rights.)

(Georgia's governor made apologies for violating the sovereignty of Tennessee and Ross was released.)

(Court's 1831 decision:

"...an Indian tribe or nation within the United States is not a foreign state in the sense of the Constitution, and cannot maintain an action in the courts of The United States....")

(That Wirt was able to get a favorable verdict from the Supreme

Study Outline	Notes and Sources

Cherokees who had been sentenced to four years at hard labor by the State of Georgia for refusing to swear allegiance to the Georgia Constitution.

g. Signatures were gained by trickery and harassment on a "treaty" which gave up 7,000,000 acres for $4,500,000 to be deposited "to their credit." The Senate hastened to ratify the "treaty."

h. The "trail of tears" awaited the Cherokee, with its misery, hunger and death. Nearly a third of the nation died on the way to Oklahoma.

10. The Creeks and others met the same fate. The 1832 Treaty of Washington (which transferred title of Creek lands to the United States and for which the Creek were to receive nothing) was broken by Whites within days of its signing. An undisguised swindling operation followed, with speculators acquiring Indian lands by every conceivable scheme of force and trickery.

Court gave hope to the Cherokee cause. But the hope was short-lived, for President Jackson chose not to accept the Supreme Court's definition of law, which ruled that the Cherokee omnibus bill was unconstitutional)

(President Van Buren stated in his 1838 message to Congress:

"...It affords me sincere pleasure to apprise the Congress of the entire removal of the Cherokee Nation of Indians to their new homes west of the Mississippi. The measures of Congress at its last session have had the happiest effects. By an agreement concluded with them...their removal has been principally under the conduct of their own chiefs, and they have emigrated without any apparent reluctance.")

Van Every, *Disinherited* (Chapter 13) (Left destitute in their own lands, Creeks were in such dire need that a few resorted to banditry, with the result that thousands were marched [many in chains] with a military escort to the West. Many perished on the way.)

11. New conflicts awaited the tribes who had removed.

    a. New treaties pledged the Five Civilized Tribes exclusive, everlasting possession of the communally owned domains, pledging that their tribal governments would be left in authority forever.

    b. During the Civil War, a majority of the Five Civilized Tribes joined the Confederate side. After the war, though the Southern States were restored to their rights and property without prejudice, Congress cancelled every treaty with their Indian allies.

(New treaties required the surrender of all their lands in the western Indian Territory. Other tribes from the woodlands and plains were settled on some of this land; the rest was thrown open to white settlement.)

    c. The Five Civilized Tribes still retained nearly 20,000,000 acres in eastern Oklahoma. Annual reports of Commissioners of Indian Affairs and debates in Congress for a number of years revolved around the knotty problem of how to take this land away from the Indians within forms of the law and without becoming involved in new Indian wars.

Collier, <u>Indians of the Americas</u> (Killing Indians was very expensive; between 1862 and 1867, wars with the Sioux, Cheyenne, and Navajo alone had cost the government $100,000,000.)

d. The "land allotment" system was one solution. Each individual received an allotted acreage. "Excess" acreage was then sold to white settlers. As private owners, the Indians could then sell their own lands if they wished. In about 20 years, all except 1,500,000 acres of the 16,000,000 originally allotted to members of the Five Civilized Tribes had passed into white hands.

(The local looting of Indians became a principal business in Eastern Oklahoma.)

12. The Plains Indian Wars

a. In 1849 the government purchased Fort Laramie from its fur-company owners and garrisoned it with troops. Then in 1851 some 10,000 Indians were gathered from all parts of the plains for a council. David Mitchel, Superintendent of Indian Affairs, headed the Washington commissioners whose purpose was to secure guarantees of safety for Whites on the Oregon Trail and to end warfare among the tribes on

Josephy, "Crazy Horse, Patriot of the Plains," The Patriot Chiefs

Storm, Seven Arrows (Deals with culture, lifestyle and traditional stories of Plains Indians as well as conflicts with Whites.)

Grinnell, The Fighting Cheyenne (In exchange, Mitchel offered government annuities and promised that soldiers at the forts to be

Study Outline	_Notes and Sources_

the plains so that Whites could
live in greater safety. Conquering
Bear signed for the Sioux, as he
had been designated "head chief" by
Mitchel.

b. In 1854 near Ft. Laramie, a Sioux
had killed and skinned a cow which
had wandered from a Mormon emigrant
company. The owner appealed to the
Army for help. J. L. Grattan, a
junior officer, summoned Conquering
Bear to the fort, where the chief
offered to pay for the cow.
Through faulty translation of a
drunken interpreter, a misunder-
standing led to violence. Grattan
took a detachment of men and two
howitzers to the Sioux village to
arrest the guilty Indian. The
frightened Indian would not submit
to arrest, so Grattan and his men
opened fire on the village, fatally
wounding Conquering Bear in the
first howitzer blast. The Sioux
warriors immediately annihilated
Grattan and his men.

erected would safeguard Indian
rights.)

Sandoz, Crazy Horse (Grattan
had boasted that with ten soldiers he could whip the entire
Cheyenne nation, and with thirty
he could make all the tribes of
the plains run.)

(Josephy and Grinnel give some-
what different versions of this
incident.)

(The Grattan incident broke the
1851 treaty. Indians no longer
felt constrained from raiding.)

Study Outline	_Notes and Sources_

c. General W. S. Harney's 1855 retaliatory raid on the Sioux camp at Ash Hollow was a typical Army action in several respects: individuals supposedly at fault were not in the camp when the raid occurred; a friendly camp was found and attacked, with the slaughter of its inhabitants to provide a "lesson."

(After that fight Harney moved to Ft. Laramie and demanded the surrender of the "murderers" of Grattan. In response, five Indians rode into camp singing their death songs.)

d. In 1856 Harney forced the Sioux to sign a new treaty requiring them to remain at peace.

e. In 1857 the first collision between Cheyennes and Whites occurred over four horses which Cheyennes had found on the prairies. White owners wanted the horses and the Indians were offered a reward, which they agreed to accept. Two Tails (later Little Wolf) refused to bring in one of the horses because he had not found it at the place and time described by the supposed owner. The Army commandant ordered some of the

(Following precedent set at the 1851 treaty, Harney designated Chief Bear Ribs to sign the treaty as "representative of all the Sioux.")

(All Wolf Fire's possessions were confiscated when his family fled his lodges. Wolf Fire

Study Outline	_Notes and Sources_

Cheyennes arrested; Wolf Fire was caught and held and another Cheyenne was killed as the remaining Indians made their escape.

f. In 1862 the Sioux uprising in Minnesota under Little Crow alarmed Whites. At the same time, some of the Indians who had aligned themselves with the Confederacy made threatening moves in Colorado. In the plains area there was really little violence in the Civil War era. A few impetuous young Kiowas were giving some trouble to the Whites.

g. Smallpox and hunger were taking a toll among the Plains Indians. Already the buffalo were becoming scarce because of hunting pressure from Whites who killed them for hides and tallow.

h. In 1864 a number of military actions against the Cheyenne were based on fictitious charges and hearsay evidence.   Colonel J. M.

himself died in the guardhouse.) (This action was followed by incidents on both sides.)

Roddis, Indian Wars of Minnesota Porter, Battle of the 1,000 Slain (Chapter 6) Abel, The American Indian as Participant in the Civil War (Indians were also rendering distinguished service in that war.)

(H. T. Ketchum, special agent who was vaccinating Indians, found some who were reduced to the necessity of eating emigrants' cattle that had died of disease.)

(Early in this campaign Black Kettle had stopped a battle after Colorado Militia opened fire on a peaceful Cheyenne group.)

Study Outline	Notes and Sources

Chivington and other Coloradans began a concerted war against the Cheyenne.

i. Chivington and his men conducted their slaughter of Black Kettle's peaceful village of Cheyennes and Arapahoes at Sand Creek that same year despite Black Kettle's American flag. Two-thirds of the victims were women and children. One officer testified later that Chivington had given the order to "kill all, little and big." At an investigation in 1865, Lt. Olney swore that he witnessed a fellow officer shoot and scalp three women and five children who had been captured.

(The movie Soldier Blue is based in part on the Sand Creek massacre.)

Brown, Bury My Heart at Wounded Knee

Hoig, The Sand Creek Massacre

Grinnell, The Fighting Cheyenne

(Soldiers took over 100 Cheyenne and Arapaho scalps to Denver, where they were greeted as heroes as they displayed their trophies between acts of a theatrical performance.)

(In his first report of the raid, Chivington said of his men that "All did nobly.")

j. Indians retaliated with raids on wagon trains, ranches, stage stations, and government stockades. Telegraph poles were destroyed. Indians attacked Julesburg and burned the town. The Sioux joined the Cheyenne in seeking revenge.

Dodge, Our Wild Indians (A reading of Colorado newspapers of the day reveals that more deaths and property losses were occurring regularly because of lawless miners and frontiersmen

Study Outline	Notes and Sources
	than were caused by all of Colorado's Indians. Indians received most of the headlines, though.)
k. In July of 1865, Indians around Fort Laramie were gathered up and given a military escort--into the country of their dreaded enemies, the Pawnees!	(Crazy Horse responded to pleas for help with a large party of warriors, killing the military commander and freeing most of the 1500 to 2000 Indians.)
l. The Powder River expedition that same year ended in frustration for the Americans, who were reduced to near starvation.	Grinnell, The Fighting Cheyenne (A number of Indians distinguished themselves in action against the Whites, Crazy Horse and Roman Nose among them.)
m. In the 1866 Battle of Fort Kearney, 79 American soldiers and two civilians, with Captain W. J. Fetterman in command, were killed by a large force of Sioux, Cheyennes, and Arapahoes. Fetterman's disobedience of orders and arrogant disdain of Indians brought about his own downfall.	Josephy, The Patriot Chiefs Andrist, The Long Death Brown, Bury My Heart at Wounded Knee (Fetterman had boasted, "Give me 80 men and I will ride through the whole Sioux Nation." Oddly, he had just that number as he rode out, so confidently that
(1) The Indians had prepared their trap well. Using their strategy to good effect, they lured Fetterman and his men to their	two civilians joined him to test their new repeating rifles--and, by coincidence, to make up his "80 men.")

Study Outline	*Notes and Sources*

annihilation.

(2) Following the "Fetterman
Massacre," and the "Wagon Box"
fight, American troops were
withdrawn from the Bozeman Trail
for a time.

n. In the Beecher Island Fight of
1868, Roman Nose was killed when he
went into battle despite not
having undergone the purification
ritual after his medicine was
broken.

o. In the Battle of the Washita,
Custer led troops against still-
peaceful Black Kettle killing him
and many of his band in a surprise
attack. Survivors joined the
Powder River hostiles.

p. In 1872 Crazy Horse and Sitting
Bull led attacks against troops
escorting a Northern Pacific rail-
road survey party, forcing them to
abandon their work. (In 1873
Custer and the 7th Cavalry managed
to get the survey parties through

(An interesting fact is that of
the 81 Whites killed, only six
died from gunshot wounds, and two
of those were possibly self-
inflicted.)

(The "Wagon Box" fight demonstrated the superiority of new
repeating rifles.)

Berger, Little Big Man

(Col. E. W. Wynkoop, who had
been involved in two Indian
massacres through no fault of
his own, resigned as agent to
the Cheyennes and Arapahoes in
protest of Custer's massacre of
the sleeping village on the
Washita.)

Sitting Bull, "Our People are
Blindly Deceived," in Witt and
Steiner's The Way

despite clashes with Crazy Horse
and his men.)

q. In 1874 Custer led an expedition
of 1200 men to gather military
and scientific information about
the Black Hills.

(The expedition violated the
1868 treaty which Red Cloud had
signed.)

(1) The United States wanted the
valuable Black Hills for Whites,
so a campaign was begun to get
the proper number of signatures
on an official document making
the cession. Imaginative pressures were applied.

(Not even Crazy Horse could stop
the rush of miners when Custer
made it known that there was gold
in the Black Hills.)

(A minor scandal broke out in
Washington when it was learned
that some prominent Sioux visi-
tors had government-paid tours
which included visits to "Bad
Houses.")

(2) In 1875 a commission met with
some 20,000 Indians at the Red
Cloud Agency for the purpose of
getting the Indians' land.

(Crazy Horse stayed away, but a
member of his band threatened

(3) The chiefs finally told the commissioners that they would sell
if the commissioners would meet
their price (Red Cloud asked
$600,000,000) and feed and
clothe the Sioux for seven
generations.

to kill the commissioners.)

(When the Sioux refused a
$6,000,000 offer, the commissioners
angrily reported to Washington
that the Sioux should be taught
a lesson. Late that year, at
President Grant's instigation,

r. Half of General George Crook's
command attacked Two Moons'

the Indian Office ordered all
hostile Indians to come into the

Study Outline	_Notes and Sources_

Cheyenne village, taking the Cheyenne by surprise. Colonel J. J. Reynolds, who was in charge of the six attacking companies, was forced to retreat when the Cheyenne counterattacked. Crook was forced to abandon the campaign for that winter as a result.

s. Crook called the 1876 Battle of the Rosebud a victory for his troops, and it is so recorded in most histories.

t. The change in plans necessitated by Crook's withdrawal caused some rearrangement of troops under Gibbon and Terry. The next important event was Custer's battle with a large force of Indians on the Little Big Horn River. The Indians won.

u. In 1876 following Custer's defeat, Red Cloud's village was captured near Fort Robinson. Dull Knife's village was then attacked by a combined force of Indians and white soldiers. After escaping to cover,

agencies by January 31 or be driven in by troops.)

Sandoz, Crazy Horse

(Because of the attack, Two Moons, who had been preparing to go into the agency, changed his plans and joined Crazy Horse.)

Grinnell, The Fighting Cheyennes

(Grinnell, who recorded versions of the battle related to him by Indian participants, regarded the Indians as the victors.)

Neihardt, "The Ru-bing Out of Longhair," Black Elk Speaks

Chief Eagle, Winter Count

Josephy, "The Custer Myth," Life, LXXI (July 2, 1971)

Smith, The Indians Won

(An interesting idea for a "what if" novel, but the book contains a number of historical inaccuracies and misconceptions.)

(In 1877 Dull Knife and his people surrendered and were taken to the hot and humid Indian territory,

Study Outline	_Notes and Sources_

Dull Knife and his band saw their village and their winter food · supply burned.

v. Though Crazy Horse held out for a time, and was actually never defeated, the Sioux were coming to the end of their military power.

  (1) In the spring of 1877 Crazy Horse went to Fort Robinson to negotiate for an agency for his tribe.

  (2) Eager to get Indian allies to help defeat other Indians, Crook asked Crazy Horse to help him fight the Nez Percé who were then making their brilliant march toward freedom.

  (3) Crook had Crazy Horse spied upon by Indians of Red Cloud and No Water's faction, who reported erroneous information to him, which caused Crook to arrest Crazy Horse.

w. As the Sioux were being escorted to the Missouri River, some 2000 who had fought with Crazy Horse left

where many starved or died from sickness.)

(Iron Plume had surrendered after being wounded. Other Sioux groups had gone in to the agencies as pressure was concentrated upon the Sioux alone. Miles' winter warfare against Crazy Horse saw the Indians eventually use all their ammunition and supplies. The hostile Sioux who remained were starving and freezing.)

(Crazy Horse finally agreed to fight the Nez Percé until not one was left; but the interpreter [who may have been conspiring with Red Cloud] translated his words to say that he would kill all the white men.)

(Crazy Horse resisted imprisonment and was killed by a sentry's bayonet while being held by other Indian guards.)

64

the columns and raced away to the

north in a successful bid for free-

dom with Sitting Bull in Canada.

x. Dull Knife and Little Wolf led   Sandoz, Cheyenne Autumn

their band in an epic 1000 mile   Grinnell, The Fighting Cheyenne

journey across the prairies back   Andrist, The Long Death

to their northern homeland. In   Fast, The Last Frontier

four major engagements their 60 to

70 men outfought and outmaneuvered

American troops, successfully

bringing their women, children and

aged back to their ancestral lands,

despite special troop trains, the

telegraph, and some 13,000 American

troops trying to prevent them. At

the end of the trek, after the

Cheyenne had split, they met strange

fates. Little Wolf eventually

joined General Miles in his cam-

paign against the Sioux. At Fort

Robinson Dull Knife's group were

imprisoned and denied food, water

and heat for days. On January 9,

1879, Dull Knife's people,

starving, freezing, and mad with

thirst, broke from their prison

with a few hidden weapons. Many
were killed or wounded in the escape; a small party managed to
hold off four companies of soldiers
for several days before they were
finally shot down, to end the war
with the Cheyennes.

y. The "Ghost Dance craze" found the
    Whites more "crazed" than the
    Indians.

    (1) Sitting Bull was murdered on
        suspicion that he was planning
        an uprising among the Ghost
        Dancers.

    (2) In 1890 American soldiers con-
        ducted the last "war" against
        the Plains Indians when they
        killed almost 300 Indian men,
        women and children at Wounded
        Knee. In the melee some 60
        soldiers were killed or wounded,
        mostly by their own men (though
        a few of the unarmed Indians had
        managed to get weapons).

13. The Nez Percé campaign of 1877 was
     preceded by white encroachment upon

Bailey, Wovoka

Brown, Bury My Heart at Wounded
Knee
Andrist, The Long Death
Porter, Battle of the 1,000 Slain
Neihardt, "The Butchering at
Wounded Knee," Black Elk Speaks
(Black Elk was at the scene before the shooting stopped. He
described a gulch at the site:
"...it was one long grave of
butchered women and children and
babies, who had never done any
harm and were only trying to run
away.")

(When gold was discovered on the
Clearwater in 1860, miners agreed

66

Indian lands in violation of

treaties.

a. Lewiston's newspaper, the <u>Golden</u>

<u>Age</u>, advised that settlers should

ignore treaties (such as the 1855

Nez Percé treaty which established

reservations for the tribes) and

help themselves to Indian lands.

In Boise, a newspaper carried the

suggestion that smallpox-infected

blankets should be distributed to

the Nez Percé.

b. A new treaty, which was negotiated

in 1863, was signed by the Chris-

tian Lapwai Nez Percé, ceding the

lands of the Wallowa Nez Percé.

(1) The government in return was to

pay the moving expenses of the

Wallowa people to the Lapwai

reservation and to provide

training in farming methods.

(2) A number of the Wallowa people

were not too pleased at the

prospects of changing from well-

to-do ranchers to subsistence

not to go onto the Indian lands

south of the river; but immediately

they proceeded to violate their

agreement. In 1862 miners killed

three Indians, but Nez Percé

chiefs were ignored when they

asked for justice.)

Beal, <u>I Will Fight No More Forever</u>

(a fairly objective and detailed

account of incidents leading to

the war and of the campaign it-

self)

(Yellow Wolf, Young Joseph's

nephew, said that the Lapwai

group "sold our homes. Sold our

country which they did not own.")

(The Lapwai reservation could not

support the extensive herds of

cattle and horses owned by the

Wallowa Nez Percé.)

farmers. The 1863 treaty marked

the end of Nez Percé unity.

(3) The Wallowa tribe steadfastly

refused to part with their

homeland.

c. A series of legal decisions and in-   (The Wallowa reservation had

creasing pressures from settlers   shrunk to about one-fourth of

led up to an extremely reluctant   its 1855 size of some 4,500,000

agreement to remove to Lapwai to   acres by 1877.)

sixty plots of twenty acres each

which had been set aside for them.

(1) The Wallowas were given sixty   (Many animals were lost in the

days to round up their animals   move, as some escaped in the

and to cross the Snake River   hurried roundup and as Whites

and the Salmon to their new   seized the opportunity to drive

home.   off cattle and horses.)

(2) No human lives were lost in the

crossing of the flood-swollen

Snake River.

d. Acting on their own, without tribal   (Several of the whites killed by

sanction, a small group of young   the young Nez Percés had mur-

Nez Percés made the overt acts   dered Indians and had not been

which led to war, killing a number   punished under white law.)

of Whites.

e. General O. O. Howard took the   Josephy, "The Last Stand of Chief

troops which had come to enforce   Joseph," The Patriot Chiefs

Study Outline	Notes and Sources

removal in pursuit of Young

Joseph's band. A number of

memorable encounters followed:

the battles of White Bird Canyon;

the Clearwater; the Big Hole; Camas

Meadows; and Bear Paws.

14. There were a number of other con-

flicts in the West and Southwest.

a. In 1878 there was the Bannock

Indian War in Idaho, Washington

Territory and Wyoming Territory,

with another indiscriminate

slaughter of women and children at

Bear River, according to reports

of white civilians.

b. The Utes of Colorado ended up

losing their lands after a pub-

licity campaign led by politicians

and newspapermen.

(1) William Vickers wrote in a

Denver Tribune editorial:

The Utes are actual, practical
Communists and the government
should be ashamed to foster and
encourage them in their idleness
and wanton waste.

(2) Where some earlier Indian war

scares in Colorado were

Notes and Sources column:

U.S. Army, American Military
History, 1607 to 1953 (p. 287)

(The Army R.O.T.C. manual sum-

marizes the campaign:

"In 11 weeks he [Joseph] had
moved his tribe 1,600 miles,
engaged 10 separate U.S. com-
mands in 13 battles and skir-
mishes, and in nearly every
instance had either defeated
them or fought them to a
standstill.")

Madsen, The Bannock of Idaho

Brown, "The Utes Must Go," Bury

My Heart at Wounded Knee

(In 1879 the article was reprinted

throughout Colorado under the

title "The Utes Must Go." And

in 1881 the Utes were marched 350

miles to a reservation in Utah.)

Dodge, Our Wild Indians

described by some Army officers
as merely ballyhoo for the purpose of insuring a military post
in an area for businessmen to
sell to, the 1879 campaign became a deliberate land grab.

c. An 1875 expedition against Indians
in Eastern Nevada was characterized by misunderstandings and
frontier overeagerness and bravado.

d. The Apaches, superb guerilla   Salaz, "The Race," El Grito, IV
fighters, fought Mexicans and,   (Winter 1971), 22-23.
later, Americans in sporadic vio-
lence over a period of many years.

   (1) Cochise, Victorio, Nana, Mangas   (Unscrupulous businessmen and
        and Geronimo were names made   traders fanned the embers of war
        famous in the Southwest when   when the flames were low--to keep
        White settlers became desirous   the military handy as a market
        of additional lands.   and to create a greater demand

   (2) In 1886 General Miles with 500   for their goods among the Indians.)
        Apache scouts and 5000 soldiers
        were in the field after Geron-
        imo. That year, at last,
        Geronimo surrendered.

e. The Treaty of Guadalupe Hidalgo   (From the first, government repre-
bound the United States to pacify   sentatives made a distinction in

Study Outline	Notes and Sources

the Navajos and Apaches, who had been raiding Pueblo and Mexican villages for many years.

policy toward the Indians: the Pueblos were to be cultivated peacefully; the Navajos and Apaches were to be dealt with militarily.)

f. In 1858 at Fort Defiance trouble broke out when the Army seized a large area of Navajo grazing land.

(1) The post commander ordered Navajo horses grazing on the disputed land to be shot.

(2) Navajos retaliated by shooting the commander's Negro slave.

(A punitive expedition merely aroused Barboncito, Herrero and Manuelito to attack the fort itself with a party of 2000 warriors.)

g. The Navajos interpreted the American withdrawal from Fort Defiance at the start of the Civil War as a sign of weakness. Accordingly, the Navajos attacked white settlements.

(1) Then in the 1860's General James H. Carleton devised a utopian Indian removal scheme.

(2) Kit Carson became the field commander to carry out the removal scheme.

(3) Whenever he met resistance, he destroyed crops, rounded up herds and shot the Navajo men.

(Carleton had been sent to New Mexico in 1863 to repel the Confederates, who had already left the territory.)

(Carson had previous success against the Mescalero Apaches.)

(Carson's destruction of the peach orchards was an especially bitter memory.)

Study Outline	*Notes and Sources*

(4) On March 6, 1864, over 2000 Navajos began the "Long Walk" to Bosque Redondo. Some 8500 were eventually removed to Bosque Redondo, where conditions were extremely bad.

(5) The 1868 treaty allowed the Navajos to return to a new reservation in part of their former homeland.

15. The forces which California Indians struggled with represent a cross-section of the conflicts faced by most American Indians, though the results were in some ways more frightening or more immediate than usual.

   a. In California, the Indian mission era spanned a period of about one human lifetime. The Padres, well-intentioned and devoted to duty as they may have been, hastened the doom of their Indians. Most of the tribes that were devoted to Mission life are long extinct. At Santa Barbara after 13 years of the

Underhill, The Navajos

Keleher, Turmoil in New Mexico 1846-1868

(Carleton's plan was a failure: a number of Navajos eluded capture and removal; many deserted the camp at Bosque Redondo; in 1867 the Navajos refused to plant crops; and in 1868 the Bosque Redondo scheme was abandoned.)

Kroeber, Ishi in Two Worlds

Collier, The Indians of the Americas

Jackson, Ramona

Stafford, "The Concealment: Ishi, the Last Wild Indian," The Reserved Year

Atherton, "The Vengeance of Padre Arroyo," in Simmen's The Chicano

Study Outline	Notes and Sources

mission system, there were 864 living Indians; 662 Indians had died. After 1834, when the missions ended, the mission Indians died at an increasing rate.

Kroeber and Heizer, Almost Ancestors: The First Californians

b. There were 110,000 to 130,000 Indians in California in 1850. By 1880 fewer than 20,000 remained. Disease took many; enslavement caused some deaths; white soldiers did their duty to wipe out some; and white "sportsmen" took a toll (killing Indians was not regarded as murder).

Porter, Battle of the 1,000 Slain (Chapter 9)
Miller, "Blood on the Snow," in Anderson and Wright's The Dark and Tangled Path
(Joaquin Miller's 1890 tale is a strong indictment of frontier violence against native Americans in California.)

c. The United States negotiated treaties with 119 tribes, with the Indians surrendering more than half of the state of California (there were no negotiations with tribes occupying the other half) and accepting in return, perpetual ownership of 7,500,000 acres.

(Californians exerted pressure and the Senate never ratified any of these treaties. The result was that all of the land guaranteed to the Indians was also sold to Whites.)

d. Indians fulfilled their part of the agreement, but they soon found themselves dispossessed, with only meaningless treaties to show for

(The Indian Bureau, "guardian" of the tribes, kept very quiet about what had happened to the treaties.)

their claims to half of Calif-

ornia.

III   Conclusion

   Though there were other outbreaks of anti-White or anti-Indian violence
after the 1890 incident at Wounded Knee, such as the Leech Lake Chippewa
disturbances in 1898, such actions were on a minor scale. Removal to reservations had still not stopped the ambitions of Whites to acquire Indian lands,
under one pretext or another.

   The Indians faced still other conflicts, most of which developed out of
white efforts to "civilize" the red man or to "integrate" him into a mono-
cultural America. Such conflicts find a place in this volume in the "Identity"
and "Nationalism and Integration" sections.

   Though the Indian fought his neighboring tribe, he did so at least partly
in the attitude of sport. It is true that inter-tribal warfare was serious;
it determined hunting rights and tribal territorial boundaries. And those
who fought were often killed. But Indian warfare lacked the machine-like
efficiency and the sustained intensity which Whites brought to the battlefield.

   At least a part of the effectiveness of the Indian in battle with the White
is due to the fact that he was defending his home and his family. Whites, on
the other hand, were the aggressors in the action. They were attacking the
Indian in his home, killing his women and children as well as the warrior himself. Fighting for his very existence, for his children (who were there at
his side) and for his religion and his way of life, the Indian was capable of
a desperate courage.

PART THREE: INDIAN NATIONALISM VERSUS INTEGRATION

I   Introduction

With a number of exceptions, Indians themselves have generally pursued nationalistic rather than integrationist goals. The main form of Indian nationalism has revolved around the tribal culture. Tribalism, as Deloria points out, is an enduring force. A product of the tribal culture, the Indian finds identity and self-expression within the extended family pattern of the culture and within the tribal organization rather than as a single individual in a mass society.

There have been attempts made by able leaders to unite Indians into a nation or force extending beyond tribal lines. Some regional confederations were highly successful. A few leaders such as King Philip, Pontiac, Tecumseh and Crazy Horse have been able to gain sufficient Indian unity to achieve notable military victories over invading white armies. But in general, such unions were not far reaching and enduring.

A recent red power movement has developed, with the goal of achieving political unity and strength among America's Indian tribes, to prevent further breaking of treaties at the expense of Indians. Red power has achieved some victories, but how successful it will be in the long run remains to be seen.

A number of tribes, as well as individual Indians, chose to cooperate with Whites, becoming Christians, adopting white practices: modes of dress, farming methods, language and customs. Historically such efforts have not been rewarded, at least if the Indians happened to own property.

Whites have conducted their own campaigns to integrate Indians. Repressive campaigns to stamp out Indian culture have been conducted by churches and governmental agencies, in an effort to "civilize" the "heathen." Indian culture, including tribalism, continues to endure despite the efforts of Whites to shape the Indian into white patterns.

II   Guide and Sourcebook

Study Outline	*Notes and Sources*
A. In general, those Indians who pursued integrationist courses received no more favorable treatment at the hands of	

Whites than did those who ardently

opposed integration.

1. Massasoit made great concessions of
    land to the Whites in order to live
    at peace and in order to obtain the
    advantages of white technology for
    his people.

2. The Powhatans were friendly to the
    Virginians until they saw all their
    lands being taken. But the Powhatans
    were to lose their tribal strength
    forever then they opposed further
    white encroachment.

3. The Praying Indians of New England
    had accepted Christianity and aided
    the Puritans against Philip.

4. The Iroquois were already possessed
    of a government system which served
    in part as a model for later United
    States governmental processes. They
    made commercial ties with the colo-
    nists and on occasion **sided** with the
    colonists in war, as integrationist
    gestures.

5. The Delawares, who were defrauded of
    most of their best lands in Thomas

Josephy, The Patriot Chiefs

(Whites who had acquired most of
Massasoit's lands were still not
content, nor were they ready to
accept Indians into their own
society as equals.)

(Pocahontas even married one of
the Virginians.)

(This course did not result in
their gaining admittance into
white society on an integrated
basis.)

Jackson, A Century of Dishonor

(The author makes much of the

Study Outline	*Notes and Sources*

Penn's sly <u>Walking Purchase</u>, became "civilized," accepting white culture, becoming farmers and Christians. Their integrationist efforts seemed quite successful for a time. Then Whites massacred a number of them; and others were **forced** to remove to the West because Whites wanted their lands.

Delawares' Christianity and peaceful and successful agricultural pursuits as she tells in some detail of white injustice to the Delawares and others.)

6. The Five Civilized Tribes of the Southeast had begun to adopt the white man's ways before they were forced to accept President Jackson's removal plan.

Van Every, <u>Disinherited</u> (This book has much detail on the Five Civilized Tribes.)

  a. The Choctaw of Mississippi had intermarried with Whites. Some had become successful planters and merchants.

  b. The Chickasaws had a long record of friendliness to the United States.

(Chickasaws had aided the U.S. in wars against northern Indians.)

  c. The Seminoles were a peaceful group with whom runaway slaves found asylum and with whom they integrated.

Van Every, <u>Disinherited</u> (See the note from William Bartram's <u>Travels</u>.)

Study Outline	*Notes and Sources*

d.   The Creeks had aided the United States in wars against other Indians.

e.   The Cherokees had adopted the white man's clothes along with his religion, Christianity. (They were to follow a course of passive resistance to removal.)

(Individual Cherokees became planters, millowners, businessmen and printers. A number of them intermarried with Whites.)

f.   Though all these acts may be regarded as gestures toward integration, they proved ineffectual when Whites desired the Indians' lands.

(See, for example, the story of Tsali of the Cherokees in Marriott and Rachlin's American Indian Mythology.)

7.   There were other similar examples elsewhere.

a.   The Pawnees were consistently helpful to the Whites in the Indian wars of the West, serving as guides and warriors in the United States military forces.

(When the wars ended, the Pawnees were removed to live with the other Indians with whom they had fought.)

b.   Many Nez Percés accepted Christianity. Some of them became peaceful farmers at Lapwai. And some became successful breeders of quality livestock in their Wallowa Valley and mountains.

(Despite their having accepted white ways, those who had extensive herds and land were forced onto small plots which might support only a vegetable garden and perhaps a cow or two.)

Study Outline	Notes and Sources
8. Indians have experienced the personal conflicts which arise as a result of trying to retain Indian identity in a white man's world, or as a result of attempting to gain acceptance from Whites who are reluctant to recognize the human potential or worth of the Native American.	Momaday, House Made of Dawn LaFarge, Laughing Boy Oberly, "The Intellectual Tribal Leader..." in Witt and Steiner's The Way LaFarge, The Enemy Gods Cushman, Stay Away, Joe Wilson, Apologies to the Iroquois Borland, When the Legends Die Waters, The Man Who Killed the Deer Jayne, Old Fish Hawk McNichols, Crazy Weather Corle, Fig Tree John
9. Some function very successfully in the white man's world, though not necessarily because they have accepted the Anglo Saxon value system.	Udall, Me and Mine (Account of a Hopi mother whose family have achieved successes scholastically and in trades and professions.)
10. Some have achieved because of their own outstanding talents which carried them to heights of success.	Wilson, Apologies to the Iroquois (The Philip Cooks whom Wilson describes are an interesting and apparently successfully integrated family.)
11. Some Indians have urged an integrationist course for Indians in recent years. a. Louis R. Bruce, an Onondaga who is a successful New York City businessman and who was for a time	(Bruce's stance at the Trail of Broken Treaties protest probably strengthened his standing in the

Study Outline	*Notes and Sources*
President Nixon's Commissioner of Indian Affairs, is regarded by some Indians as being an apple (red outside and white inside).	eyes of many Indians, though it cost him his office.)
b. W. W. Keeler, the able businessman and Cherokee leader, is also considered by some to be too white.	(Though Keeler is head chief of the Cherokees, that office--like a number of other similar positions--is filled by white appointment.)
c. Dr. Ben Reifel, a former congressman of Indian descent, has been an advocate of what many see as integrationist goals.	(Reifel's address to the Northern Montana Work Conference on Indian Education, November 27, 1956, was strongly integrationist in tone.)
B. Tribalism has been the dominant form of Indian nationalism.	Van Every, Disinherited
1. Typically each tribe, whether large or small, regarded itself as a distinct entity or nation.	("The basic Indian weakness in coping with the ever-growing threat to their existence as a people was from the outset their failure to recognize the community of their interests as a people," p. 23.)
2. While such an arrangement created possibilities for individuality, it did little to help the overall Indian cause against the Whites.	
3. Tribalism created as much distrust of other Indians as of Whites.	(See part B of the "Conflict" section other details and sources on tribalism.)

Study Outline	*Notes and Sources*
4. Whites took advantage of Indian differences and enmities to further their own cause in their wars of aggression against Indians.	Steiner, The New Indians (The author points to a trend away from Indian disunity.)
5. Even today tribalism persists, sometimes at the expense of overall benefits to Indians.	Deloria, Custer Died for Your Sins (pp. 220-221) (Deloria also points out the values of
6. Tribalism has positive features and values. It is the culture of tribalism which has made it possible for the Indian to succeed in their struggle for existence as a people.	tribalism.) Collier, Indians of the Americas Thomas, "On an Indian Reservation ..." in Witt and Steiner's The Way Deloria, We Talk, You Listen Waters, The Book of the Hopi Waters, Pumpkin Seed Point

C. Aside from well-organized Indian nations in Mexico and South America, there were some attempts to achieve a larger than tribal Indian unity in what is now the United States. Some leaders were more or less successful in achieving a unity which went across tribal lines. Such larger alliances scored notable military victories against the United States.

1. The Iroquois confederation of five tribes were sufficiently organized

Josephy, The Patriot Chiefs

and had sufficient strength that
Whites were extremely reluctant to
engage them in war.

2. King Philip was successful in gaining
   Indian allies to the Wampanoag cause.
   Had it not been for the integrationist Praying Indians and for the
   Mohegans and Pequots, traditional
   enemies of the Wampanoags, his war
   would very likely have been successful and the Whites would have been
   swept from New England (however
   temporarily).

3. In Canada, Brant achieved a degree
   of success as a coalition leader.

4. Pontiac's successes and failures
   fluctuated with the success of his
   pleas for unity against the Whites.
   At the height of his military success, he had a number of Indian
   allies aiding his own tribe.

5. Little Turtle, the Miami chief whose
   defeat of General St. Clair was
   actually a larger Indian victory than
   that of Crazy Horse over Custer, was
   successful in gaining Shawnee and

Colden, The History of the Five
Indian Nations

Brant, "Restore to Us Our Country,"
in Witt and Steiner's The Way
(See the "Conflict" unit for some
details on the success of these
leaders in war against Whites.)
Pontiac, "Live as Your Wise
Fathers Lived Before You," in Witt
and Steiner's The Way

Delaware allies (among others) in his efforts to defeat the Whites.

6. Tecumseh was perhaps the most successful of all who attempted to unite all Indians against the Whites. He united many Indian tribes to the overall cause, including Blackhawk of the Sac and Fox, and such distant Indians as the Tallassees and Creeks of the South.

Tecumseh, "The Way...Is for All the Redmen to Unite," in Witt and Steiner's The Way

7. Black Hawk, who tried to unite the Indians of the Midwest against the Whites, had very little success. He was opposed by Keokuk in his own tribe; and in other tribes he failed to attract any significant numbers to his cause.

Black Hawk, "He Drank the Blood of Some Whites," and Keokuk, "Our New Home Will Be Beyond a Great River," in Witt and Steiner's The Way

8. The most notable alliance of tribes in the West was that of the Sioux, Cheyenne, Arapahoe and others, which, under Red Cloud, won the Powder River War and under Crazy Horse's leadership, achieved several victories over Whites, including the defeat of Custer on the Little Big Horn.

(Later, Red Cloud and his Agency Indians represented the opposing integrationist impulse among the Sioux.)

(It should also be noted that the Navajo Nation also presented a large unified front against U.S. troops.)

D. Laws and treaties made by Whites have defined the nationalistic or integrationist status of Indians.

    1. In 1763 when the French and Indian War ended, England recognized Indian rights and established a formal policy for dealing with Indians.

    2. The "Northwest Territory Ordinance" of 1787 adopted the 1763 English Royal Proclamation as policy of the United States.

    3. In 1803, $3,000 was appropriated to civilize and educate the "heathens." And in 1819 a "civilization fund" was established for the same purpose with an annual appropriation of $10,000.

    4. A Bureau of Indian Affairs was established in the War Department in 1824.

    5. In 1828 in the **case** of Worcester vs. The State of Georgia, a court ruling held that Indian tribes were sovereign nations and not subject to state laws.

    6. In 1834 the Indian Trade and Intercourse Act allowed the Army to quarantine Indians so that they could

Jackson, A Century of Dishonor

Deloria, Custer Died for Your Sins

(The 1763 treaty stated in part:

"The utmost good faith shall always be observed towards the Indian, their lands and property shall never be taken from them without their consent and their consent and their property, rights and liberty shall never be invaded or disturbed.")

Steiner, The New Indians

(Apaches and Navajos were subjected to this quarantine in 1864

84

Study Outline	*Notes and Sources*
20. The 1968 Civil Rights Act allows reliance on traditional Indian solutions to problems only to the extent that they do not conflict with state and federal laws.	Deloria, Custer Died for Your Sins (p. 234)
E. Christianity and education were almost forced upon Indians as means of "civilizing" or integrating them.	Franklin, excerpt from Concerning the Savages of North America, in Anderson and Wright's The Dark and Tangled Path
1. For many years Whites exercised what might be described as a religious imperialism over Indians. Indian reservations were divided up among some of the Christian churches. The government assigned the Indian reservation to a particular church, with the specified denomination to exercise a territorial "sovereignty" (recognized by the other churches selected by the government to participate in the scheme) over the reservation "colony."	LaFarge, The Enemy Gods Wilson, Apologies to the Iroquois Collier, The Indians of the Americas Deloria, "Missionaries and the Religious Vacuum," Custer Died for Your Sins Steiner, "The Great White Father Myth," The New Indians Borland, When the Legends Die Mitchel, Miracle Hill Momaday, A House Made of Dawn
2. Sacred rites of the Indians considered "pagan" or "heathen" were prohibited. While the Constitution guaranteed religious freedom, that freedom was interpreted as not	Ladd, Chunda (This white missionary novel might be read for its negative descriptions of Navajos who practice their own "ungodly" religion.

applying to anything but certain

approved Christian forms for Indians.

3. As a part of their responsibility,
the churches undertook the education
of the Indians to the language and
culture of the Whites. (Later the
government's Indian schools were
taken out of the hands of denomina-
tional religions.)

4. Many of the Whites who were involved
as missionaries or teachers were
sincerely interested in helping the
Indians. But many of these Whites
were also quite intolerant of Indian
culture and values. Often the Whites
brought with them a "spare the rod
and spoil the child" philosophy which
was utterly foreign to the Indian.
Indian students were sometimes actually kidnapped to attend boarding
schools. There they were regimented
in dormitory life, perhaps forbidden
to use their native language on pain
of punishment, or of being kept on in
the school when vacation time came.
Indians who were products of white

Its tone is perhaps too typical
of the Indians' experience with
Whites. The central characters,
a young Navajo boy and girl, are
taught to despise the Navajo
culture, as all "good" Navajos
should.)

"My Teacher Is a Lizard: Educa-
tion and Culture," in Witt and
Steiner's The Way
(Several selections are Indians'
reactions to schools.)
Warrior, "Which One Are You? Five
Types of Young Indians," in Witt
and Steiner's The Way
Waters, The Man Who Killed the
Deer
Momaday, House Made of Dawn
Platero and Miller, "Chee's
Daughter," in Momaday's American
Indian Authors

schools or who were strongly influ-
enced by Anglo culture often found
themselves at odds with their tribes-
men.

F. The recently begun Red Power Movement   "The Long Road," in Witt and
crosses lines of tribal nationalism,   Steiner's The Way (Contains
aiming for a unity of all Indians in   several selections which are
claiming their rights guaranteed by   relevant to this section.)
treaties (which continue to be broken
under every national administion).

1. A number of organizations and Indian
leaders have worked to bring about
justice for Indians in America.

a. In 1925 the Indian Defense League   Wilson, Apologies to the Iroquois
was founded by Clinton Richard, an   (By some strange quirk Indians
Iroquois, to provide a defense fund   had been classified officially
for Indians who could not afford   as "Orientals" and forbidden
legal aid. The Legal Defense   to cross the border--or, pre-
League's first victory came in re-   sumably, denied re-entry.)
establishing the rights of Indians
(guaranteed under the Jay Treaty of
1794) to travel freely back and
forth across the U.S.-Canadian
border.

b. The oldest continuous Indian-run
organization is the League of

Nations, Pan American Indians. The League of Nations seeks a return to traditional Indian customs.

c. The National Congress of American Indians, which has been described as an "Indian United Nations," was founded in 1944. Among its leaders have been Vine Deloria, Jr., John Belindo, Earl Old Person, and Lee Cook.

(The NCAI has concerned itself with reservation Indians.)

d. The National Indian Youth Council, which Deloria describes as the "SNCC of Indian Affairs," was organized in 1961 by a group of ten young Indian leaders. Prominent among these were Melvin Thom, a Nevada Paiute; Clyde Warrior, a Ponca who had worked with SNCC in Mississippi; and Herbert Blatch-ford.

Thom, "The New Indian Wars," in Witt and Steiner's The Way (The NIYC has also worked to improve conditions for urban Indians.)

e. During the Poor People's March on Washington, Indian participants formed an alliance called the Coalition of American Indian Citizens. That March failed to attract support of a majority of Indians.

f. The Urban American Indian Protest Committee, headed by Mary Thunder and George Mitchel, was organized in Minnesota's Twin Cities to protest the Bureau of Indian Affairs' policy of ignoring urban Indians.

Witt and Steiner's, The Way (Several selections in Part III relate to the problems faced by urban Indians.)

g. More recently, leaders of the American Indian Movement (AIM) have become involved in helping non-reservation Indians. Russell Means, a national coordinator of AIM, met with other Indian leaders in an Off-Reservation Indian Coalition meeting in Omaha in early 1972.

(AIM has been active in promoting a number of Indian causes, participating in the Trail of Broken Treaties protest march on Washington and the 1973 protest at Wounded Knee, on Pine Ridge reservation. See the Indian Newspaper Akwesasne Notes for good coverage of these two events.)

h. There are a number of other organizations which are devoted to regional issues or to particular interests, such as publication.

Deloria, Custer Died for Your Sins (The author discusses a number of such organizations.)

2. Indian protests at continued treaty breaking or at inequities or injustices have been expressed in a variety of ways.

(A 1971 television program, a "fictional" treatment of an almost identical situation, came out with a "moderately-happy,"

Study Outline	*Notes and Sources*
a. In the late 1950's the Tuscaroras battled for their reservation, which New York officials wanted to flood for a power dam. After nearly losing their reservation to the somewhat dubious tactics of the Power Authority, the Tuscaroras took their case to the courts and continued to resist all offers for their homeland. In 1959 the Tuscaroras secured a federal ruling in their favor. (Other Indian reservations continue to be in demand for damsites and other uses valuable to Whites.)	obviously <u>WHITE</u> liberal ending in which the tribe agrees to give up its reservation for the dam-site, and in return is promised modern housing on a nearby game preserve "for twenty years." The white, liberal good-friend-to-the-Indians-type who has secured such liberal terms for them says something about having purchased the Indians a little time. Presumably once they are off the TV camera they use that twenty years to achieve the integration which 350 years has not yet accomplished.)
b. Wallace "Mad Bear" Anderson, a Tuscarora, led a delegation from the Six Nations of the Iroquois to Cuba in 1959 to request that Cuba sponsor admission of the Iroquois to the United Nations as a sovereign and independent state.	Wilson, <u>Apologies to the Iroquois</u> (Wilson explores the high-handed methods used by Robert Moses and the Power Authority of the State of New York against the Tuscaroras, and the Tuscaroras' action in return.)
c. In 1963 South Dakota's Sioux, led by William Whirlwind Horse and Cato Valandra, held voter registration	(State senator James Ramey, who had sponsored the legislation, was also defeated in the election.)

Study Outline	*Notes and Sources*

drives and succeeded in getting out 90% of eligible Sioux voters to defeat the passage of a law which would have placed Indian lands under state jurisdiction (and indirectly made them available to Whites).

d. At the 1964 Washington State fish-in, sponsored by the National Indian Youth Council, a number of young Indians demonstrated to assert traditional tribal fishing rights. Alvin James Bridges, Janet McCloud and others led the protesting fisherman. Robert Satiacum, Bruce Wilkie, Mel Thom and Marlon Brando made speeches at the state capitol. Some two and a half years after the Indians began their fish-ins, the Department of Justice appeared before the Washington State Supreme Court on behalf of a tribe which had been enjoined from exercising its treaty fishing rights.

(Melvin Thom, a Nevada Paiute leader, was president of NIYC at the time.)

(The State of Washington had barred the Quinalts from their traditional fishing grounds and had leased the fishing rights to the Baker's Bay fishing Company for $36,000 a year. With the building of dams and with continued white encroachment, Indian landholdings in Washington State had shrunk to the point that some had no site of their own from which to pursue their traditional livelihood by fishing.)

Study Outline	*Notes and Sources*
e. The Urban American Indian Protest Committee carried protest signs as it picketted a B.I.A. area office, protesting neglect of off-reservation Indians.	Steiner, The New Indian (Steiner says, "For the government to defend the tribes' rights in a treaty made with the government was unprecedented.")
f. In 1966 John Chewie, a Cherokee, was on trial for hunting deer as part of an organized protest, and as part of an organized effort to put meat on the table. At the trial in the small town of Jay, Oklahoma, 400 armed Indians appeared.	(Annual Indian per capita income in the area was $500.)
g. In December 1971, a court decision affirmed the rights of Minnesota Chippewas, under provisions of historic treaties, to hunt, fish and harvest wild rice on public lands on their reservation without adhering to state regulations.	(These Indians had been allowed to pursue such a course on only four or five percent of their 588,000 acre reservation lands.)
h. Richard McKenzie led the "Raid on Alcatraz," to claim the abandoned prison as a site for a University of the American Indian. Indians occupied the island and its government facilities for some time	Josephy, Red Power ("We Must Hold on to the Old Ways" and Deloria, "This Country Was a Lot Better Off When the Indians Were Running It.")

Study Outline	Notes and Sources

before being evicted. In June 1971 Michael Chosa led a similar, though shorter-lived, takeover of a Chicago missile site which the federal government was no longer using.

(Chosa, an Air Force veteran and a migrant labor organizer, led other takeovers of abandoned federal properties in Wisconsin and Illinois in August 1971, to demonstrate the plight of the urban Indian.)

i. American Indian Movement leaders Russell Means of Cleveland, Dennis Banks of Washington, and Vernon Bellecourt of Denver, were instrumental in raising a force of nearly 1,000 demonstrators to protest the death of Raymond Yellow Thunder at Gordon, Nebraska. Yellow Thunder's death served as a rallying point for a large Indian demonstration against discrimination at Gordon and at nearby Pine Ridge, South Dakota.

(Yellow Thunder was allegedly stripped from the waist down, then thrust onto the dance floor at a dance in the American Legion Hall in Gordon, Nebraska. His body was found eight days after the dance, on February 20, 1972, in a used-car lot in Gordon. Rumors spread to the effect that Yellow Thunder had been tortured and mutilated. An autopsy showed that the rumors were exaggerated.)

j. The Trail of Broken Treaties protest march on Washington in late 1972 was sponsored by eight national Indian organizations, which had adopted a 20 point position paper for discussion and negotiation. Government reaction

(For the most complete and objective treatments of the Trail of Broken Treaties protest and the Wounded Knee protest which followed, see the Indian newspapers Wassaja and Akwesasne Notes. Akwesasne Notes has also published

tended to obscure the issues involved and to concentrate instead
on mere physical presence of numbers of unwanted Native Americans
in the Capitol. What started out
as an apparently peaceful protest,
turned into an angry demonstration
with Indians occupying the B.I.A.
headquarters and damaging the
building's interior. There were
Government sponsored guided tours
through the clutter for some time
before the business of cleaning up
got under way.

k. The village of Wounded Knee, South
Dakota, was occupied by members of
and others as a protest against
(1) the lack of response to the
twenty points, (2) the incomplete-
ness of negotiations and agree-
ments in the Sioux treaty meetings
of a century ago, and (3) the
allegedly despotic Indian government of the Pine Ridge Reservation.
The village was held by militant

a reprint of its coverage of
the Trail of Broken Treaties,
titled B.I.A.--We're Not Your
Indians Anymore. D'Arcy McNickle
also treats the issues involved
in his book Native American
Tribalism.)

(Several ranking officials of the
Indian Affairs Commission lost
their jobs--or were given different ones--as a result, direct
or otherwise, of the Trail of
Broken Treaties.)

(Navajo tribal chairman Peter
MacDonald revealed in a nationally
broadcast interview that government officials had pressured a
number of tribal chairmen into
denouncing the Washington protest. MacDonald claimed that
there was broad support or sym-
pathy for the protest--though
not necessarily for the destruction which accompanied it--
among Indians.)

protestors for many days against the seige of Federal Marshalls.	(Casualties at Wounded Knee included two Indians killed and one Marshall wounded in the gunfire exchanged.)

1. Larry Casuse, a Navajo student and president of the KIVA Club at University of New Mexico, was killed in a gun battle with Gallup police after he had kidnapped Mayor Emmet Garcia in March 1973.

(Casuse had kidnapped Garcia to protest his "exploitation of Indians." At Window Rock a year later a "Gathering for Humanity and Indian Awareness" was held to honor the late Casuse.)

3. As new dams are constructed, Indians lose homesites or traditional fishing grounds. Whites still cast covetous eyes on timber, minerals, land or water which belong to Indians.

Stafford, "The fish Counter at Bonneville," The Rescued Year

Deloria, Custer Died for Your Sins

a. Pyramid Lake Paiutes in Nevada fear losing the lake which supports them, as Whites continue to appropriate the water which was guaranteed to Nevada's Indians.

(Deloria says that

"more damage is being done to the Indian people today by the United States than was done in the last century.")

b. The Indian Peaks Band of Paiutes had their 10,000 acre reservation sold out from under them for a $40,000 purchase price in 1956, under the Indian policy then in effect.

Anderson, "Paiutes Our Most Deprived Indians."

(Nationally syndicated column, August 12, 1971.)

c. Thor Tollefson, director of Washington's State Fisheries, had

(To the Indian, losing his livelihood did not seem to be much progress.)

Study Outline	*Notes and Sources*

justified modern-day treaty-

breaking: "The treaty must be

broken. That's what happens when

progress pushes forward."

d. Wahleah Lujan, a Taos Indian co-ed

who was Miss Indian America, made

this statement:

"In the last twenty years we've
been pushed around a lot. Our
land is being taken away.... Our
sacred Blue Lake, the church of
our Indian religion, is being taken
away.... Land that has belonged
to no one but us. Land that my
people have been on for six hundred
and fifty years. And all of a
sudden these strange people come in
and tell us: You can't use this
land any more! It's not yours!"

Steiner, *The New Indian*

(Miss Lujan is quoted.)

"Our Indian Heritage," *Life*

(July 2, 1971)

(The lake was finally returned

to the Taos Indian tribe in

December 1970.)

e. The Indian Omnibus Bill of 1967 was

a proposed solution to the "Indian

problem." But, typically, it had

been drafted without consulting

the Indians as to their own per-

ceptions of their needs and de-

sires. Indians resented such

paternalism and the often unrealis-

tic products of such all-white

planning. The Omnibus Bill con-

tained provisions for mortgaging

Indian reservations, which Indians

Steiner, *The New Indian*

(Stewart Udall, then Secretary

of the Interior, made these

comments, which show not only

his own good intentions but also

the fact that Indians were not

allowed to help plan policies

which would affect them:

Let's give the new leadership
to the Indian people...

The spirit of Santa Fe was the
spirit of asking ourselves what
our Indian people want.

Study Outline	*Notes and Sources*

interpreted as making their lands available to Whites.

f. Apache Indians of the Rio Verde reservation in Arizona were forcibly removed to the San Carlos reservation 122 miles away and their own lands in Rio Verde were taken from them in 1872. At the turn of the century some of them returned to live on a small tract in the Tonto National Forest, near Payson, Arizona. In 1971 Milton Campbell, leader of the group, was in Washington lobbying for the rights of the Indians. The Bureau of Indian Affairs refused to recognize the Payson Apaches as Indians unless they submit to removal to the San Carlos reservation once again. The Department of Interior agreed to give title to the eighty-six acre tract they have been on since the turn of the century--on condition that they accept the title as a corporation, not as an Indian tribe.

--quoted in The New Indians p. 261.)

(It was at Santa Fe that the 1967 Omnibus Bill--which some Indians described as the Ominous Bill--was planned, without benefit of any Indian advice or participation.)

(Because they were regarded as squatters on the national forest-- where they had been for some seventy years--their legal status prevented them from bringing in electricity, running water, or a sewage system. Spiro Agnew pledged $12,500 in royalties from the sale of wristwatches to the Indian community for development, but he specified that the money not be spent unless the Apaches received title to the land. After considerable publicity, this issue was happily resolved, with these Tonto Apaches receiving title to the ground and retaining their Indian

4. American Indians are not willing to see their homes taken and their culture destroyed. They are speaking out to demand a voice in their own destiny.

   a. Representatives of thirty Indian tribes were asked to pass judgment on the proposed Omnibus Bill. Raymond Nakai and the other Indian delegates shocked Whites with their 44-5 vote against the Omnibus Bill and their counterproposal asking for massive "foreign aid" similar to that extended to emerging nations. In part the "Resolution of the Thirty Tribes" stated:

> We sold our ancestral lands to the United States in return for perpetual protection through federal trusteeship. We do not expect to pay twice.

   b. Will Rogers had voiced Indian suspicions which still persist, when he made these statements on America's Indian wars:

> "You look at all Wars and you will find that that there is more new

identity--and getting Vice President Agnew's money.)

Josephy, <u>Red Power</u> ("We Have Endured. We Are Indians" and other sections)

Apapas, "We Do Not Want Any Other Home," in Witt and Steiner's <u>The Way</u>

Steiner, <u>The New Indian</u> (Commissioner Bennett had been reassuring before the Indians voted on the proposed legislation:

For the first time we are consulting with the Indians before sending legislation to Congress. This is a novel experience for them, and some are hesitant. But the whole intent is to bring the Indians more into the decision-making process.)

deeds for land signed at these
peace conferences than there is
good will."

"...in Wars the Slogan is Honor,
but the object is land."

"They are always fighting for
Independence, but at the finish
they always seem to be able to
use quite a snatch of the defeated
opponent's land to be Independent
on."

c. Mel Thom had described a major

    problem with government policies:

    "The people who are our bosses tell   Steiner, The New Indian
    us what we want. And that's what
    we end up with. I've yet to see
    Indians getting in on top policy-
    making."

    Thom defined relocation as,

    "dumping the rural poor into the
    ghettoes."

d. Alyce Williams, Yurok leader:

    "Our Big Brother, our protector,   Steiner, The New Indian
    the Bureau of Indian Affairs, says
    it is the 'Helper' of the Indians.
    But its actual mission has been to
    take away [the voice] of the In-
    dians, to control the Indians, and
    to keep the Indians out of the
    white man's hair."

e. Lisa Waukau:

    "The whites are hypocrites. Why   Steiner, The New Indian
    do the whites always talk about
    what Hitler did to the Jews? They
    don't know what they are talking
    about. They did the same thing to
    us. They slaughtered most of us,
    but that didn't satisfy them; now
    they want to steal what we have
    left."

Study Outline	_Notes and Sources_

f. Excerpt from an editorial in <u>NCAI</u>
    <u>Sentinel</u>:

    "To wistfully look to the Oliver
    La Farges for counsel is sheer
    folly today as events are moving
    too fast in American history to
    have Indians take a back seat in
    decision-making in favor of a 'wise
    all-knowing' white friend. Yet let
    us not kid ourselves, the Oliver
    La Farges are still around and
    increasing everyday. They appear
    whenever and wherever there are
    problems, programs, and activity.
    They still seek to influence and
    counsel and end up creating con-
    fusion."

g. Clyde Warrior:

    "The natives were always restless
    and so the Bureau and its Uncle
    Tomahawks were always trying to
    calm the natives down. It has been
    their job throughout history."

h. Wallace "Mad Bear Anderson (after
    his return from Cuba in 1959):

    "This is the dawn of a new day. I
    will do all in my power to see
    Indians unite across the continent.
    There is a movement of Indian
    nationalism in the nation."

i. Vine Deloria, Jr.:

    "Red power will win. We are no
    longer fighting for physical sur-
    vival. We are fighting for ideo-
    logical survival. Our ideas will
    overcome your ideas. We are going
    to cut the country's whole value
    system to shreds."

    But Deloria cautioned:

Notes and Sources (f.): "On the 'Wise All-Knowing'
White Friend," in Steiner's
<u>The New Indian</u>

Study Outline	_Notes and Sources_

"Ideological leverage is always superior to violence...violence and militancy are animalistic shortcuts to non-existent ends."

Deloria, We Talk, You Listen (p. 251)

j. Robert Thomas, Cherokee anthro-

pologist:

"Every three years there is a new generation. And every new generation is more Indian than the last. Youth leaders of the National Indian Youth Council, who were hot-shots three years ago, are considered by the new Indians to have cooled it, to be conservative.

(Thomas' point is born out by a 1961 University of Chicago study which found that

"Indian communities, as separate, distinct social systems, are increasing in population."

--quoted in McNickle's Native

American Tribalism)

k. Carter Camp, AIM leader:

We have never participated in America. Our people have never gone out to vote, because there is nothing to vote for. You shouldn't vote for the next guy who is going to rip off your people, no matter what kind of lies he tells you. The Indian people have never really accepted the United States Government's authority over their lives and their land....

From an interview reported in

Akwesasne Notes (Early Autumn,

1973, issue)

We don't need a lot of money. We don't need social status. We have to have freedom. We have to have the ability to govern our own land areas and our people. Our government has to be set up as an Indian government, and left alone by the white government so we can live in the way we want to live.

III Conclusion

Indians have learned from sad experience that they can't trust white do-gooders. The Delawares who had converted to Christianity and adopted the peaceful ways of the Moravians were massacred by their white Christian neighbors.

Following the publication of Helen Hunt Jackson's A Century of Dishonor, which painted a sad picture of white perfidy, there was a misguided but logical (from the standpoint of Mrs. Jackson's recommendations) attempt to Christianize the Indian and make him fit the "American" role of independent agrarian. As a result, under the allotment system, Indians lost two-thirds of the land they then possessed. And the legal problem of heirship which arose made it impossible for many Indians of the next generation to use what land they owned. In effect, the reservations had shrunk again.

Indians had come to such a state by the early twentieth century that many believed what the social Darwinists had predicted: that the Indians would actually vanish or die out. In 1918 a high official of the Indian Bureau testified before a House investigating committee that as the Indians were being liquidated, there was no need for conservation practices on Indian lands and that Indian forests should be cut clean.

When Collier was Commissioner of Indian Affairs, he had liberal and humane ideals as he helped bring about a much improved federal Indian policy. But even his well-intended efforts were not without negative side effects. In his efforts to institute conservation practices on the Navajo reservation, he actually created hunger and poverty where none had existed before.

A number of Indians, especially the young, are expressing their dissatisfaction with colonial status and their impatience with the fact that Indians have almost never been consulted in the development of programs designed by the government for Indians. Indians are demanding a voice in working out their own affairs.

Indians do not wish to become white men. Their own cultures are flexible enough to fulfill their needs even in the twentieth century. They are asking that treaty obligations be fulfilled and that they be allowed to maintain their tribal or individual Indian identities.

Indian Bibliography

Abel, Annie H. The American Indian as Participant in the Civil War. (2
    vols.) Cleveland: Arthur H. Clark, 1919.

Allen, T. D. Navajos Have Five Fingers. Norman: University of Oklahoma,
    1963.

Anderson, Jack. "Paiutes Our Most Deprived Indians," (Nationally syndi-
    cated column), August 12, 1971.

Andrist, Ralph K. The Long Death. New York: Macmillan, 1964.

Astrov, Margot, editor. American Indian Prose and Poetry. Gloucester,
    Massachusetts: P. Smith, 1970.

Bailey, Lynn R. Indian Slave Trade in the Southwest. Los Angeles:
    Westernlore, 1966.

Bailey, Paul. Wovoka. Los Angeles: Westernlore, 1970.

Baity, Elizabeth C. Americans Before Columbus. New York: Viking, 1951.

Baldwin, Gordon C. America's Buried Past: The Story of North American
    Archaeology. New York: E. P. Putman, 1962.

_____. Games of the American Indian. New York: W. W. Norton, 1969.

Ballotti, Geno Arthur. A Survey of Prose Literature About the Southwest
    Indian. Unpublished M.A. Thesis, University of Wyoming, 1955.

Beal, Merrill D. I Will Fight No More Forever. New York: Ballantine,
    1971.

Berger, Thomas. Little Big Man. Greenwich: Fawcett, 1970.

Berthrong, Donald J. The Southern Cheyennes. Norman: University of
    Oklahoma, 1963.

Bird, Harrison. Battle For a Continent. New York: Oxford University,
    1965.

Bleeker, Sonia. The Sioux Indians, Hunters and Warriors of the Plains.
    New York: William Morrow, 1962.

Borland, Hal. When the Legends Die. Philadelphia: J. B. Lippincott, 1969.

Bradford, William. Of Plymouth Plantation, edited by Harvey Wish. New York:
    Capricorn, 1962.

Brandon, William. American Heritage Book of Indians. New York: Dell, 1961.

_____. "American Indian Literature," Indian Historian, IV (Summer 1971), 53-55.

Britt, Albert. Great Indian Chiefs. Freeport, New York: Books for Libraries, 1969.

Britton, Wiley. The Union Indian Brigade in the Civil War. Kansas City, Missouri: Franklin Hudson, 1922.

Brody, J. J. Indian Painters & White Patrons. Albuquerque: University of New Mexico, 1971.

Brophy, William A., and Sophie D'Aberle. The Indian America's Unfinished Business. Norman: University of Oklahoma, 1968.

Brown, Dee Alexander. Bury My Heart at Wounded Knee. New York: Bantam, 1972.

Brown, Joseph Epes. The Sacred Pipe. Baltimore: Penguin, 1971.

Cahn, Edgar S., editor. Our Brother's Keeper: The Indian in White America. New York: World, 1970.

Capps, Benjamin. The White Man's Road. New York: Ace Books, 1969.

Chief Eagle, D. Winter Count. Denver: Golden Bell, 1968.

Clark, Ella. Indian Legends from the Northern Rockies. Norman: University of Oklahoma, 1966.

Coffin, Tristram P., editor. Indian Tales of North America. Philadelphia: American Folklore Society, 1961.

Cohen, Felix. Handbook of Federal Indian Law. Washington, D.C.: United States Government Printing Office, 1945.

Colden, Cadwallader. History of Five Indian Nations. Ithaca: Cornell University, 1969.

Collier, John. Indians of the Americas. New York: New American Library, 1971.

Cooke, David C. Fighting Indians of the West. New York: Dodd, Mead, 1954.

_____. Indians On the Warpath. New York: Dodd, Mead, 1957.

Corkran, D. H. The Cherokee Frontier. Norman: University of Oklahoma, 1962.

Corle, Edwin. Fig Tree John. New York: Liveright, 1971.

_____. People on the Earth. New York: Random House, 1937.

Cory, David M. Within Two worlds. New York: Friendship Press, 1955.

Costo, Rupert, editor. Textbooks and the American Indian. San Francisco: Indian Historian, 1970.

Cotterill, R. S. The Southern Indians. Norman: University of Oklahoma, 1954.

Council on Interracial Books, Chronicles of American Indian Protest. Greenwich: Fawcett, 1971.

Covarrubias, Miguel. The Eagle, the Jaguar and the Serpent; Indian Art of the Americas. New York: Alfred Knopf, 1954.

Cronyn, George W. American Indian Poetry. New York: Ballantine, 1972.

Cummings, Byron. First Inhabitants of Arizona and The Southwest. Tucson: Cummings Publications Council, 1953.

Cummins, Lawrence E. "Hope for the American Indian?" Ensign, I (July 1971), 14-18.

Cunningham, Frank. General Stand Watie's Confederate Indians. San Antonio: Naylor, 1959.

Curtis, Natalie. The Indians Book. New York: Dover, 1969.

Cushman, Dan. Stay Away, Joe. Great Falls, Montana: Stay Away, Joe Publishers, 1968.

Dale, Edward E. Indians of the Southwest. Norman: University of Oklahoma, 1949.

David, Jay, editor. The American Indian: The First Victim. New York: Morrow, 1972.

Day, A. Grove. The Sky Clears. Lincoln: University of Nebraska, 1951.

Debo, Angie. A History of the Indians of the United States. Norman: University of Oklahoma, 1970.

_____. And Still the Waters Run. Princeton: Princeton University, 1940.

Deforest, John W. History of the Indians of Connecticut. Hamden, Connecticut: Shoe String, 1964.

Deloria, Ella. Speaking of Indians. New York: Friendship Press, 1944.

Deloria, Vine, Jr. Custer Died for Your Sins. New York: Avon, 1970.

_____. We Talk, You Listen. New York: Macmillan, 1970.

Densmore, Frances. Chippewa Customs. (Bureau of American Ethnology Bulletin 86.) Washington D.C.: United States Government Printing Office, 1929.

DeRosier, Arthur H., Jr. Removal of the Choctaw Indians. Knoxville: University of Tennessee, 1970.

Dodge, Colonel Richard Irving. Our Wild Indians. Freeport, New York: Books for Libraries, 1970.

Dorian, Edith. Hokahey! American Indians Then and Now. New York: McGraw, 1957.

Douglas, Frederic H. and Rene d'Harnoncourt. Indian Art of the United States. New York: Arno, 1969.

Downey, Fairfax. Indian Fighting Army. New York: Scribner's, 1944.

Driver, Harold E. Indians of North America. Chicago: University of Chicago, 1970.

_____, and Wilhelmine Driver. Indian Farmers of North America. Chicago: Rand McNally, 1967.

Dunn, Dorothy. American Indian Painting of the Southwest and Plains Area. Albuquerque: University of New Mexico, 1969.

Dunn, Jacob P., Jr. Massacres of the Mountains: A History of the Indian Wars of the Far West. New York: Capricorn, 1969.

Dyk, Walter, recorder. Son of Old Man Hat. Lincoln: University of Nebraska, 1966.

Eastman, Charles A. From the Deep Woods to Civilization. Boston: Little, Brown, 1916.

_____. Indian Boyhood. New York: Dover, 1971.

_____. Old Indian Days. New York: Fenwyn Press, 1970.

_____. Soul of an Indian. New York: Dover, 1970.

Embree, Edwin Rogers. Indians of the Americas. New York: Collier, 1970.

Embry, Charles B. America's Concentration Camps: The Facts About Our Indian Reservations Today. New York: McKay, 1956.

Emmitt, Robert. The Last War Trial. Norman: University of Oklahoma, 1954.

Ewers, John C. Indian Life on the Upper Missouri. Norman: University of Oklahoma, 1968.

Fall, Thomas. The Ordeal of Running Standing. New York: Bantam, 1971.

Feldman, Susan, editor. The Story Telling Stone: Myths and Tales of the American Indian. New York: Dell, 1965.

Fey, Harold Edward, and D'Arcy McNickle. Indians and Other Americans. New York: Harper and Row, 1970.

Fiedler, Leslie. Return of the Vanishing American. New York: Stein and Day, 1969.

Finger, Charles Joseph. Tales From Silver Lands. Garden City: Doubleday, 1937.

Forbes, Jack D. The Indian in America's Past. Englewood Cliffs: Prentice Hall, 1964.

_____. Nevada Indians Speak. Reno: University of Nevada, 1967.

Foreman, Grant. Last Trek of the Indians. Chicago: University of Chicago, 1946.

_____. The Five Civilized Tribes. Norman: University of Oklahoma, 1966.

_____. Indian Removal. Norman: University of Oklahoma, 1953.

_____. Indians and Pioneers. Norman: University of Oklahoma, 1967.

_____. Sequoyah. Norman: University of Oklahoma, 1970.

Forrest, Earl R. Missions and Pueblos of the Old Southwest. Cleveland: Arthur H. Clarke, 1929.

Forrest Williams. Trail of Tears. Norman: University of Oklahoma, 1959.

Fritz, Henry Eugene. The Movement for Indian Assimilation, 1860-1890. Philadelphia: University of Pennsylvania, 1963.

Geronimo. Geronimo: His Own Story, edited by S. M. Barrett. New York: Ballatine, 1970.

Garcia, Andrew. Tough Trip Through Paradise. New York: Ballantine, 1968.

Gessner, Robert. Massacre. New York: Da Capo, 1972.

Gibbens, Euell. Stalking the Wild Asparagus. New York: David McKay, 1971.

Glassley, Ray H. Pacific Northwest Indian Wars. Portland, Oregon: Binfords and Mort, 1953.

Grey, Herman. Tales from the Mojaves. Norman: University of Oklahoma, 1970.

Griffin, James Bennett, editor. <u>Archaeology of Eastern United States</u>. Chicago: University of Chicago, 1952.

Grinnell, George Bird. <u>The Fighting Cheyennes</u>. Norman: University of Oklahoma, 1971.

_____. <u>Pawnee, Blackfoot and Cheyenne</u>. New York: Scribner's, 1961.

_____. <u>Pawnee Hero Stories and Folk-Tales</u>. Lincoln: University of Nebraska, 1961.

_____. <u>When Buffalo Ran</u>. Norman: University of Oklahoma, 1969.

Hackett, Charles W. <u>Revolt of the Pueblo Indians of New Mexico</u>. Albuquerque: University of New Mexico, 1942.

Hagan, William T. <u>American Indians</u>. Chicago: University of Chicago, 1951.

_____. <u>The Sac and Fox Indians</u>. Norman: University of Oklahoma, 1958.

Haines, Francis. <u>Indians of the Great Basin and Plateau</u>. New York: Putnam, 1970.

_____. <u>The Nez Percés</u>. Norman: University of Oklahoma, 1955.

Hamilton, Charles, editor. <u>Cry of the Thunderbird</u>. New York: Macmillan, 1951.

Hamilton, Edward P. <u>The French and Indian Wars: The Story of Battles and Forts in the Wilderness</u>. Garden City: Doubleday, 1962.

Henry, Jeannette, editor. <u>American Indian Reader: Anthropology</u>. San Francisco: Indian Historian, 1972.

_____. <u>American Indian Reader: Education</u>. San Francisco: Indian Historian, 1972.

_____. <u>American Indian Reader: Literature</u>. San Francisco: Indian Historian, 1973.

Hertzberg, Hazel W. <u>The Search for an American Indian Identity</u>. Syracuse, New York: Syracuse University, 1971.

Hodge, Frederick Webb. <u>Handbook of American Indians North of Mexico</u>. (Bureau of American Ethnology Bulletins 31 and 32), Washington, D.C.: United States Government Printing Office, 1907-1910.

Hoffman, Charles, editor. <u>War Whoops and Medicine Songs</u>. Boston: Boston Music Co., 1952.

Hoig, Stan. <u>The Sand Creek Massacre</u>. Norman: University of Oklahoma, 1961.

Hopkins, Sarah Winnemucca. Life Among The Piutes. (Edited by Mrs. Horace Mann.) Boston: 1883.

Hough, Henry W. Development of Indian Resources. Denver: World Press, 1967.

Howard, Oliver O. My Life and Experiences Among Our Hostile Indians. New York: Plenum, 1969.

Hunt, W. Bernard. Golden Book of Indian Crafts and Lore. New York: Golden Press, 1954.

Irving, Washington. Astoria. (2 vols.) Philadelphia: J. B. Lippincott Co., 1961.

_____. A Tour on the Prairies. Norman: University of Oklahoma, 1971.

Isely, Mary. Uncommon Controversy. Seattle: University of Washington, 1970.

Jackson, Helen H. A Century of Dishonor. Minneapolis: Ross and Haines, 1964.

_____. Ramona. New York: Avon, 1970.

James, Ahlee. Tewa Firelight Tales. New York: Longmans Green, 1927.

Jayne, Mitchell F. Old Fish Hawk. New York: Pocket Books, 1971.

Johnson, Dorothy M. A Man Called Horse. New York: Ballantine, 1970.

Josephy, Alvin M. Nez Perce Indians and the Opening of the Northwest. New Haven: Yale University, 1968.

_____. The Indian Heritage of America. New York: Alfred Knopf, 1968.

_____. The Patriot Chiefs. New York: Viking, 1969.

_____. Red Power. New York: American Heritage, 1972.

Kappler, Charles J. Laws and Treaties. Volume 2 (Treaties) Washington, D.C.: U.S. Government Printing Office, 1904.

Keiser, Albert. The Indian in American Literature. New York: Octagon, 1970.

Keleher, William A. Turmoil in New Mexico 1846-1868. Santa Fe: Rydal, 1952.

Kelly, William H. Indians of the Southwest. Tucson: University of Arizona, 1953.

Kirk, Richard, and Clara L. Tanner. Our Indian Heritage. Chicago: Follett, 1962.

Klein, Bernard, and Daniel Icolari, editors. Reference Encyclopedia of the American Indian. New York: B. Klein, 1967.

Kneale, A. H. *Indian Agent*. Caldwell, Idaho: Caxton, 1960.

Knight, Oliver. *Following the Indian Wars*. Norman: University of Oklahoma, 1960.

Kopit, Arthur. *Indians*. New York: Bantam, 1971.

Kroeber, Theodora. *Ishi in Two Worlds*. Berkeley: University of California, 1961.

_____, and Robert F. Heizer. *Almost Ancestors: The First Californians*. New York: Ballantine, 1970.

LaBarre, Weston. *The Peyote Cult*. New York: Schocken, 1969.

Ladd, Horatio O. *Chunda*. New York: Eaton and Mains, 1906.

LaFarge, Oliver. *As Long as the Grass Shall Grow*. New York: Longmans, Green, 1940.

_____. *The Enemy Gods*. Boston: Houghton Mifflin, 1937.

_____. *Laughing Boy*. New York: New American Library, 1971.

Laubin, Reginald. *The Indian Tipi*. New York: Ballantine, 1971.

Lauritzen, Jonreed. *Arrows into the Sun*. New York: Alfred Knopf, 1943.

Lawton, Harry. *Tell Them Willie Boy Is Here*. New York: Award Books, 1969.

Leach, Douglas Edward. *Flintlock and Tomahawk: New England in King Philip's War*. New York: Macmillan, 1958.

Leon, Robert L. "Mental Health of Indian Boarding School Children," *Emotional Problems of Indian Students in Boarding Schools*: Workshop Proceeding, Albuquerque, New Mexico, 1960.

Levine, Stuart, and Nancy O. Lurie, editors. *The American Indian Today*. Baltimore: Penguin, 1970.

Lewis, T. M. N., and Madeline Kneberg. *Tribes that Slumber*. Knoxville: University of Tennessee, 1958.

Lincoln, Charles H. *Narratives of the Indian Wars, 1675-1699*. New York: Scribner's, 1913.

Linderman, Frank B. *Plenty-Coups: Chief of the Crows*. Lincoln: University of Nebraska, 1962.

_____. *Red Mother*. New York: John Day, 1932.

Link, Margaret S., compiler. *The Pollen Path*. Stanford: Stanford University, 1956.

governments of the Five Civilized

Tribes.

14. Congress passed a law providing for

    citizenship to all Indians.

15. The 1934 Wheeler-Howard Act (Indian   (The Wheeler-Howard Act provided

    Reorganization Act II) was passed,   each tribe the right to have its

    allowing tribes to incorporate with   own charter and its own constitu-

    the government.   tion and the right to plan its

16. In 1940 Congress provided for   own development.)

    naturalization procedures for Indians

    to become citizens.

17. In 1946 Congress established the

    Indian Claims Commission, providing

    legal means for compensation to

    Indian tribes for loss of lands.

18. In 1953 Congress adopted the Hoover   (Under provisions of the Termina-

    Commission's 1949 recommendation   tion Law, states were to be

    that some tribes be terminated from   allowed to take over jurisdiction

    federal trusteeship.   of Indian lands. Indian prohibi-

19. There has been a government retreat   tion was also stopped.)

    from the termination and relocation   Ortiz, "On the Road, Indian-Style

    policies which have been very un-   ..." and Old Person, "The Main-

    popular with Indians.   stream..." in Witt and Steiner's

                                                  The Way

assimilate and take their place in
the mainstream of American life.

7. In 1894 the Bureau of Indian Affairs
was transferred to the Interior
Department.

8. In 1854 Congress provided for lands
to be placed in trust for the Indians
after cession of other tribal lands
to the government.

9. In 1871 Congress stopped all treaty
making with Indian tribes. Indian
tribes were declared "domestic, de-
pendent nations."

10. In 1878 Congress provided for Indian
Police.

11. Courts of Indian Offences were established in 1883.

12. In 1887 the Dawes Severalty Act
(Allotment Act) was passed, to divide
up tribal lands to individuals, and
to provide for sale of "excess" lands
to Whites.

Marriott, "Allotments," The Ten
Grandmothers

13. In 1898 the Curtis Bill was enacted
into law providing for land allotment
and for dissolution of the tribal

Linton, Ralph, editor. <u>Acculturation in Seven American Indian Tribes</u>. New York: Appleton-Century, 1940.

Lockwood, Frank C. <u>The Apache Indians</u>. New York: Macmillan, 1938.

Lowie, Robert H. <u>Indians of the Plains</u>. New York: Doubleday, 1963.

Lurie, Nancy Oestreich, editor. <u>Mountain Wolf Woman</u>. Ann Arbor: University of Michigan, 1966.

Lyback, Johanna. <u>Indian Legends of Eastern America</u>. Chicago: Lyons and Carnahan, 1963.

Lyford, Carrie Alberta. <u>The Crafts of the Ojibwa (Chippewa)</u>. Phoenix: Phoenix Printing Department, 1943.

McCombe, Leonard, Evon Z. Vogt, and Clyde Kluckhohn. <u>Navaho Means People</u>. Cambridge: Harvard University, 1951.

McGaa, Ed. "A Bigoted Textbook," <u>The Indian Historian</u>, IV (Fall 1971), 53-55.

McNichols, Charles L. <u>Crazy Weather</u>. Lincoln: University of Nebraska, 1967.

McNickle, D'Arcy. <u>The Indian Tribes of the United States</u>. New York: Oxford University, 1962.

_____. <u>Native American Tribalism</u>. New York: Oxford University, 1973.

_____. <u>Runner in the Sun</u>. New York: Holt, Rinehart and Winston, 1954.

_____. <u>They Came Here First</u>. Philadelphia: J. B. Lippincott, 1949.

Madsen, Brigham D. <u>The Bannock of Idaho</u>. Caldwell, Idaho: Caxton, 1958.

Marquis, Thomas B., interpreter. <u>Wooden Leg</u>. Lincoln: University of Nebraska Press, 1967.

Marriott, Alice. <u>Sequoyah, Leader of the Cherokees</u>. New York: Random House, 1956.

_____, and Carol K. Rachlin. <u>American Epic</u>. New York: New American Library, 1970.

_____. <u>American Indian Mythology</u>. New York: Thomas Y. Crowell, 1968.

_____. <u>Peyote</u>. New York: Thomas Y. Crowell, 1971.

Marriott, Alice Lee, editor. <u>Winter-Telling Stories</u>. New York: Thomas Y. Crowell, 1968.

Martin, Paul Sidnew. <u>Indians Before Columbus</u>. Chicago: University of Chicago, 1947.

Mathews, John Joseph. Wah'Kon-Tah, The Osage and the White Man's Road. Norman: University of Oklahoma, 1968.

Mead, Margaret. The Changing Culture of an Indian Tribe. New York: Columbia University, 1932.

Means, Florence Crannell. Our Cup Is Broken. Boston: Houghton Mifflin, 1969.

Meriam and Associates. The Problem of Indian Administration. Baltimore: Johns Hopkins, 1928.

Meyer, William. Native Americans: The New Indian Resistance. New York: International, 1971.

Mishkin, Bernard. Rank and Warfare Among The Plains Indians. New York: J. J. Augustin, 1940.

Mitchel, Emerson Blackhorse, and T. D. Allen. Miracle Hill. Norman: University of Oklahoma, 1967.

Momaday, N. Scott. House Made of Dawn. New York: New American Library, 1969.

_____. The Way to Rainy Mountain. New York: Ballantine, 1970.

Momaday, Natachee Scott, editor. American Indian Authors. Boston: Houghton Mifflin, 1972.

Mooney, James. The Ghost-Dance Religion, and the Sioux Outbreak of 1890. Chicago: University of Chicago, 1965.

Moorehead, Warren K. The American Indian in the United States, Period 1850-1914. Andover, Massachusetts: Andover Press, 1914.

Morgan, Lewis H. League of the Ho-de-no-sau-nee or Iroquois. New York: Burt Franklin, 1968.

Murphy, Marjorie N. "Silence, the Word, and Indian Rhetoric," College Composition and Communication, XXI (December 1960), 356-363.

Murray, Keith A. The Modocs and Their War. Norman: University of Oklahoma, 1959.

Nabakov, Peter, editor. Two Leggings: The Making of a Crow Warrior. New York: Thomas Y. Crowell, 1967.

Nammack, Georgiana C. Fraud, Politics, and the Dispossession of the Indians. Norman: University of Oklahoma, 1969.

National Geographic Society. Indians of the Americas. Washington, D.C., 1955.

Neihardt, John G. Black Elk Speaks. Lincoln: University of Nebraska, 1961.

_____. When the Tree Flowered. Lincoln: University of Nebraska, 1970.

Newcomb, Franc (Johnson). Navaho Folk Tales. Santa Fe, New Mexico: Santa Fe Museum of Navaho Ceremonial Art, 1967.

Nowell, Charles James. Smoke From Their Fires, edited by Challan S. Ford. New Haven: Yale University, 1958.

Nye, Wilbur S. Carbine and Lance: The Story of Old Fort Sill. Norman: University of Oklahoma, 1958.

Oehler, C. M. The Great Sioux Uprising. New York: Oxford University, 1959.

O'Kane, Walter C. The Hopis: Portrait of a Desert People. Norman: University of Oklahoma, 1953.

_____. Sun in the Sky. Norman: University of Oklahoma, 1970.

Ortiz, Alfonso. The Tewa World. Chicago: University of Chicago, 1969.

Oswalt, Wendell H. This Land Was Theirs: A Study of the North American Indian. New York: Wiley, 1960.

"Our Indian Heritage," Life, LXXI (July 2, 1971).

Owen, Roger C., James F. Deetz and Anthony Fisher, editors. The North American Indians: A Source-Book. New York: Macmillan, 1967.

Parkman, Francis. The Conspiracy of Pontiac. New York: E. P. Dutton, 1962.

Parsons, Elsie Worthington (Clews), editor. American Indian Life. Lincoln: University of Nebraska, 1967.

_____, editor. Kiowa Tales. New York: Kraus Reprint, 1969.

_____. Taos Pueblo. New York: Johnson Reprint, 1970.

_____. Taos Tales. New York: Kraus Reprint, 1969.

_____. Tewa Tales. New York: American Folk-Lore Society, 1926.

Pearson, Keith L. "Watch Out, You Might Assimilate," Natural History, LXXX (June-July 1971), 24-33.

Peckham, Howard H. Pontiac and the Indian Uprising. New York: Russell and Russell, 1970.

Prucha, Francis Paul. American Indian Policy in the Formative Years. Lincoln: University of Nebraska, 1970.

Rachlis, Eugene. *Indians of the Plains*. New York: American Heritage, 1960.

Radin, Paul, editor. *Autobiography of a Winnebago Indian*. New York: Dover, 1963.

Reichard, Gladys A. *Dezba, Woman of the Desert*. New York: Augustin, 1939.

Relander, Click. *Drummers and Dreamers*. Caldwell, Idaho: Caxton, 1956.

Richardson, Rupert Norval. *The Comanche Barrier To South Plains Settlement*. Glendale, California: Arthur H. Clark, 1933.

Richter, Conrad. *The Light in the Forest*. New York: Bantam, 1966.

Robinson, Doane. *A History of the Dakota or Sioux Indians*. Minneapolis: Ross and Haines, 1967.

Robinson, Dorothy. *Navajo Indians Today*. San Antonio: Naylor, 1969.

Roddis, Louis Harry. *The Indian Wars of Minnesota*. Cedar Rapids, Iowa: Torch Press, 1956.

Roe, Frank Gilbert. *The Indian and the Horse*. Norman: University of Oklahoma, 1955.

Rothenberg, Jerome, editor. *Shaking the Pumpkin: Traditional Poetry of Indian North Americas*. New York: Doubleday, 1972.

Sanders, Thomas E., and Walter W. Peek, editors. *Literature of the American Indian*. New York: Glencoe, 1973.

Sando, Joe S. "White Created Myths About the Native American," *The Indian Historian*, IV (Winter 1971), 10-11.

Sandoz, Mari. *Cheyenne Autumn*. New York: Avon Books, 1971.

_____. *Crazy Horse, The Strange Man of the Oglalas*. Lincoln: University of Nebraska, 1961.

Schmeckebier, Laurence F. *The Office of Indian Affairs; Its History, Activities and Organizations*. New York: AMS, 1971.

Scott, Lalla. *Karnee*. Reno: University of Nevada, 1966.

Shakespeare, Tom. *The Sky People*. New York: Vantage, 1971.

Shaw, Anna Moore. *Pima Indian Legends*. Tucson: University of Arizona, 1969.

Silverberg, Robert. *Home of the Red Man*. New York: Washington Square Press, 1971.

Simmons, Leo W., editor. Sun Chief. New Haven: Yale University, 1963.

Smith, DeCost. Indian Experiences. Caldwell, Idaho: Caxton, 1943.

Smith, LeRoi. "The Vanished American," Ensign, I (July 1971), 19-23.

Smith, Martin. The Indians Won. New York: Belmont, 1970.

Smith, Michael T. "The History of Indian Citizenship," Great Plains Journal, X (Fall 1970), 25-35.

Sonnichsen, C. L. Mescalero Apaches. Norman: University of Oklahoma, 1958.

Spicer, Edward H. Cycles of Conquest. Tucson: University of Arizona, 1962.

_____. A Short History of Indians of the United States. Princeton: Van Nostrand Reinhold, 1969.

Stafford, William. The Rescued Year. New York: Harper and Row, 1966.

Standing Bear, Luther. Land of the Spotted Eagle. Boston: Houghton Mifflin, 1933.

_____. My People the Sioux. Boston: Houghton Mifflin, 1928.

Stands in Timber, John, and Margot Liberty. Cheyenne Memories. New Haven: Yale University, 1967.

Steiner, Stanley. The New Indian. New York: Dell, 1968.

Steiner, Stan, and Shirley Hill Witt, editors. The Way. New York: Random House, 1972.

Storm, Hyemeyohsts. Seven Arrows. New York: Harper & Row, 1972.

Superintendent of Documents, Government Printing Office. Answers to Questions About the American Indians. Washington, 1964.

Tebbel, John. The Compact History of the Indian Wars. New York: Hawthorn Books, Inc., 1966.

Thomas, Alfred Barnaby. After Coronado: Spanish Exploration Northeast of New Mexico, 1696-1727. Norman: University of Oklahoma, 1969.

Thompson, Hildegard, and Associates. Education for Cross-Cultural Enrichment. Lawrence, Kansas: Haskell Institute, 1968.

Thompson, Stith. Tales of the North American Indians. Bloomington: Indiana University, 1968.

Trenholm, Virginia Cole. The Arapahoes, Our People. Norman: University of Oklahoma, 1970.

_____, and Maurine Carley. The Shoshonis, Sentinals of the Rockies.
     Norman: University of Oklahoma, 1964.

Trobriand, Phillipe. Army Life in Dakota. Chicago: Lakeside Press,
     Donnelly and Sons, 1941.

Tucker, Glenn. Tecumseh: Vision of Glory. Indianapolis: Bobbs-Merrill,
     1956.

Turner, Catherine C. Red Men Calling on the Great White Father. Norman:
     University of Oklahoma, 1951.

Tyler, Samuel Lyman. Indian Affairs; A Study of the Changes in Policy of
     the United States Toward Indians. Provo, Utah: Brigham Young
     University, 1964.

Udall, Louise. Me and Mine. Tucson: University of Arizona, 1969.

Underhill, Ruth. The Navahos. Norman: University of Oklahoma, 1971.

_____. The Northern Paiute Indians. Lawrence, Kansas: Haskell
     Institute, 1968.

_____. Red Man's America: A History of the Indians in the United
     States. Chicago: University of Chicago, 1971.

United States Congress. Indian Education, 1969. Washington: U.S.
     Government Printing Office, 1969.

Vaillant, George C. Aztecs of Mexico, edited by Susannah B. Vaillant.
     Garden City: Doubleday, 1962.

_____. Indian Arts in North America. New York: Harper, 1939.

Van Every, Dale. Disinherited. New York: Avon, 1970.

Vestal, Stanley. New Sources of Indian History--1850-1891. New York:
     Burt Franklin, 1971.

_____. Sitting Bull, Champion of the Sioux. Norman: University of
     Oklahoma, 1969.

_____. Warpath and Council Fire: The Plains Indians' Struggle for
     Survival in War. New York: Random House, 1948.

Vogel, Virgil J. American Indian Medicine. Norman: University of
     Oklahoma, 1970.

Vogt, Evon Z., and Ethel M. Albert, editors. People of Rimrock. Cambridge:
     Harvard University, 1966.

Washburn, W-lcomb E. Red Man's Land, White Man's Law. New York: Scribner's,
     1972.

Waters, Frank. Book of the Hopi. New York: Ballatine, 1969.

_____. The Man Who Killed the Deer. New York: Pocket Books, 1971.

_____. Pumpkin Seed Point. Chicago: Swallow, 1969.

Waubageshig (Dr. Harvey McCue), editor. The Only Good Indian: Essays by Canadian Indians. Chicago: New Press, 1970.

Wellman, Paul I. Death in the Desert. New York: Macmillan, 1935.

_____. Indian Wars in the West. New York: Doubleday, 1954.

Weltfish, Gene. The Lost Universe. New York: Ballatine, 1971.

Welty, Raymond Leo. "The Indian Policy of the Army, 1860-1870," Cavalry Journal XXXVI, CXXXVIII (1927), 367-381.

Werstein, Irving. The Massacre at Sand Creek. New York: Scribner's, 1963.

Wheat, Margaret M. Survival Arts of the Primitive Paiutes. Reno: Nevada Press, 1967.

Whiteford, Andrew Hunter. North American Indian Arts. New York: Golden Press, 1970.

White Horse Eagle. We Indians. New York: E. P. Dutton, 1931.

Wight, Edgar L., David P. Weston, and Clyde W. Hobbs. Indian Land and Its Care. Lawrence, Kansas: Haskell Institute, 1968.

Wilson, Edmund. Apologies to the Iroquois. New York: Random House, 1966.

Winnie, Lucille Jerry. Sah-gen-de-oh, the Chief's Daughter. New York: Vantage, 1969.

Wissler, Clark. Indians of the United States. New York: Doubleday, 1966.

_____. Red Man Reservations. New York: Macmillan, 1971.

Wolfe, Louis. Indians Courageous. New York: Dodd, Mead, 1956.

Zimmerman, Charles Leroy. White Eagle. Harrisburg, Pennsylvania: Telegraph, 1941.